ideas

ideas

houses
casas
maisons
häuser

AUTHORS
Fernando de Haro & Omar Fuentes

EDITORIAL DESIGN & PRODUCTION

 ARQUITECTOS EDITORES MEXICANOS

PROJECT MANAGER
Valeria Degregorio Vega
Tzacil Cervantes Ortega

COORDINATION
Susana Madrigal Gutiérrez

COPYWRITER
Roxana Villalobos
Gustavo López Padilla

ENGLISH TRANSLATION
Mexidiom Traducciones

FRENCH & GERMAN TRANSLATION
Passportinternational.net

Ideas
houses · casas · maisons · häuser

© 2005, Fernando de Haro & Omar Fuentes

AM Editores S.A. de C.V.
Paseo de Tamarindos 400 B, suite 102, Col. Bosques de las Lomas,
C.P. 05120, México, D.F. Tels. 52(55) 5258 0279, Fax. 52(55) 5258 0556.
E-mail: ame@ameditores.com   www.ameditores.com

ISBN 970 - 9726 - 10 - 2

Printed in Hong Kong.

14

INDEX • INDICE

94   182   264

introduction   introducción

THE SIMPLE MENTION OF THE WORD HOUSE immediately evokes a world of images and meanings. To use a metaphor, the house is a reflection of the soul in spatial terms.

"The house shelters dreams, protects the dreamer, and allows one to dream in peace," says the French philosopher Gaston Bachelard. It is aspiration, achievement, shelter and protection, a space for feelings, emotions and creation; it represents status, wealth and heritage. The idea of a house involves a

EL SIMPLE NOMBRAR LA PALABRA CASA evoca de inmediato un mundo de imágenes y significados. Si se recurriera a una metáfora, la casa significaría un reflejo del alma en términos espaciales.

"La casa resguarda las ilusiones, protege al soñador y permite soñar en paz", dice el filósofo francés Gastón Bachelard. Es aspiración, logro, lugar de abrigo y protección, territorio propicio para los afectos, las emociones y la creación; representa posición social, patrimonio y herencia. La idea de casa implica una

introduction   einleitung

LE SIMPLE FAIT DE PRONONCER LE MOT "MAISON" évoque aussitôt un monde d'images et de significations. Si l'on utilisait une métaphore, la maison serait un reflet de l'âme en termes spatiaux.

« La maison conserve les illusions, protège le rêveur et permet de rêver en paix », dit le philosophe français Gaston Bachelard. Elle est aspiration, réussite, lieu d'abri et de protection, territoire propice aux sentiments, aux émotions et à la création; elle symbolise statut social, patrimoine et héritage. L'idée de maison suppose une

DAS NENNEN DES WORTES HAUS verursacht eine Welt von Bildern und Bedeutungen sofort. Metaphorisch, würde eine Spiegelung der Seele in Sache von Raum bedeuten.

"Das Haus bewahrt die Illusionen, schützt den Träumer und erlaubt in Frieden zu träumen", sagte der französische Philosoph Gaston Bachelard. Es ist Aspiration, Leistung, Zuflucht und Schutz, günstiges Territorium für die Zuneigungen, die Emotionen und die Schaffung; auch stellt gesellschaftliche Position,

way of understanding life and how it should be lived; it is the space of the individual and the family self, and also where one shares with friends.

The sum of housing units produces the collective dwelling which is the city, everyone's space, that of the social being. But today the cosmopolitan reality is influenced by the immense flow of information that, in large part, determines how to live life and the way every person conceives his own house. This way, ideas created and experienced by different people, perhaps distant, are mixed with local customs and travel a two-way road affecting the conception of home design.

Likewise, the accelerated development of technology has had an impact on the development of cities which has been reflected in the way to conceive of and live

manera de entender la vida y cómo vivirla; es el espacio del ser individual y familiar, y también del que convive con amigos.

De la suma de las unidades, casa resulta la morada colectiva que es la ciudad, el ámbito de todos, del ser social. Pero hoy la realidad cosmopolita está influida por el inmenso flujo de información que, en buena medida, determina la manera de entender la vida y la forma en la que cada uno concibe su propia casa. Así, las ideas creadas y experimentadas por distintos pueblos, tal vez lejanos, se entremezclan con las costumbres locales, y corren por caminos de ida y vuelta actuando sobre la concepción del diseño de una casa.

Del mismo modo, el vertiginoso desarrollo de la tecnología ha impactado en el desarrollo de las

compréhension de la vie et de la façon dont il convient de la vivre. La maison est aussi bien un espace individuel et familial qu'amical.

De la somme des unités, la maison est la demeure collective qui correspond à la ville, le territoire de tous, de l'être social. Mais de nos jours, la réalité cosmopolite est influencée par l'immense flux d'information qui détermine, en bonne partie, la compréhension de la vie et la façon selon laquelle chacun conçoit sa propre maison. Les idées créées et éprouvées par divers peuples, peut-être lointains, s'entremêlent avec les coutumes locales et parcourent des chemins d'allers et retours en agissant ainsi sur la conception du plan d'une maison.

De même, le développement vertigineux de la technologie a eu un impact sur le développement

Patrimonium und Erbe dar. Die Idee eines Hauses verwickelt einen Weg um das Leben zu verstehen und, wie es zu leben; es ist der Raum für der Mensch und seine Familie, und auch, wo man mit Freunden zusammenlebt.

Das Haus ist das kollektive Wohnen, das Gebiet für allen, für einer gesellschaftlichen Person. Im Moment wird die kosmopolitische Wirklichkeit durch die riesige Strömung von Informationen beeinflußt, daß bestimmt, der Weg um verstehen das Leben und wie jedes man ihr eigenes Haus ausdenkt. Dieser Weg, die geschaffen Ideen und erfuhr Ideen von anderen Städten, vielleicht entfernte, sie werden mit den hiesigen Sitten gemischt, und beeinflussen auf der Vorstellung vom Design eines Hauses.

Im gleichen Weg hat die wirbelnde Entwicklung der Technologie die Entwicklung der Städte

in a house. New material and building procedures, as well as countless utensils, objects and specialized equipment have changed everyday customs and the ways of living together within a house.

Moreover, the modern house expresses current values, the idea of tradition and culture, political and economic reality, technological development and the meaning of society, family and human beings. Therefore, spaces in houses from the 21st century have been adapted to the new requirements of their dwellers; today there are houses generated to meet the needs of small families, for people who live by themselves or to respond to the needs of a couple's life together.

There are also a great variety of architectural design interpretations for a house, from traditional functionalism, to organic architecture, regional movements, high-tech, deconstructivism or the minimalist variations spread throughout the world. This diversity is the result of each person's concern regarding the image and the peculiarities that each person wishes to present in his own house, and in which the application of a design process that takes into account light and color plays a fundamental role.

ciudades y se ha reflejado en la manera de concebir y vivir una casa. Nuevos materiales y procedimientos constructivos, así como una infinidad de utensilios, objetos y equipos especializados han cambiado las costumbres cotidianas y las formas de convivencia en una casa.

Asimismo, la casa moderna expresa los valores actuales de la vida, la idea de tradición y cultura, la realidad política y económica, el desarrollo tecnológico, y lo que significan la sociedad, la familia y el ser humano. Por ello, los espacios de las casas del siglo XXI se han adaptado a los nuevos requerimientos de sus moradores; hoy existen casas que se generan para cubrir las necesidades de familias poco numerosas, para quienes viven solos, o para responder a las exigencias de convivencia de una pareja.

Existe también una gran variedad de interpretaciones arquitectónicas de diseño para una casa, desde el tradicional funcionalismo, pasando por la arquitectura orgánica, los movimientos regionales, el *high-tech*, el deconstructivismo o las variantes minimalistas difundidas en todo el mundo. Esta diversidad le permite a cada persona disponer de un amplio abanico de posibilidades que pueden resolver la imagen y particularidades que desea que estén contenidas en su propia casa. Es necesaria la aplicación de un proceso de diseño racional en el que se deben tomar en cuenta las consideraciones de luz y color como elementos fundamentales.

des villes et se reflète dans la conception et la vie d'une maison. De nouveaux matériaux et méthodes de construction, ainsi qu'une infinité d'ustensiles, d'objets et d'équipements spécialisés, ont modifié les habitudes quotidiennes et la vie en commun au sein de la maison.

Aussi, la maison moderne reflète-t-elle les valeurs actuelles de la vie, l'idée de tradition et de culture, la réalité politique et économique, les innovations technologiques, et ce que signifient la société, la famille et l'être humain. C'est pour cette raison que les espaces des maisons du vingt-et-unième siècle se sont adaptés aux nouvelles demandes de leurs occupants. Il existe aujourd'hui des maisons pour couvrir les besoins de familles peu nombreuses, pour des personnes qui vivent seules, ou bien pour répondre aux exigences de vie commune d'un couple.

Il existe aussi une grande variété d'interprétations architectoniques du plan d'une maison, du fonctionnalisme traditionnel en passant par l'architecture organique, les mouvements régionaux, le high tech, le déconstructivisme ou les variantes minimalistes répandues dans le monde entier. Cette diversité est due au souci de tout un chacun quant à l'image et aux particularités souhaitées pour sa propre maison, et dans lesquelles l'application d'un processus de plan et design, en tenant compte de la lumière et des couleurs, joue un rôle fondamental.

beeinflußt, und es ist in der Vorstellung von einem Haus und Lebensstil widergespiegelt worden. Neue Materialien und konstruktive Verfahren, sowie mehrere Gebrauchsgegenstande, Gegenstände und spezialisierte Ausrüstungen haben die täglichen Sitten und Koexistenz in ein Häusern verändert.

Ebenso, der moderne Haus symbolisiert die aktuellen Werte des Leben, der Tradition- und Kultur-Idee, der politischen und wirtschaftlichen Wirklichkeit, der technologischen Entwicklung, und die Bedeutung von der Gesellschaft, der Familie und dem Menschen. Wegen dieses haben die Räume von den Häusern des XXI Jhr. die neuen Anforderungen ihrer Bewohner angepaßt; heute gibt es Häuser, die entworfen wurden, um die Notwendigkeiten kleiner Familien zu füllen, für jenen, die allein wohnen, oder um die fordert Koexistenz eines Ehepaar zu antworten.

Es gibt auch verschiedenartige architektonische Auslegungen von Design für ein Haus, zum Beispiel die traditionelle Sachlichkeit, die organische Architektur, die regionalen Bewegungen, das High-Tech, die Dekonstruktionism oder die minimalistische Varianten aus aller Welt. Diese Vielfalt ist das Ergebnis von der Sorge jeder Person über das Aussehen, und Besonderheiten enthielten in seinem eigenen Haus, und wo die Anwendung eines Designprozesses, welche betrachten das Licht und die Farbe ist wesentlich.

colour
color
couleur
farbe

TEXTURES, COLOR AND LIGHT allow the three-dimensional characteristics of space to be admired and are a fundamental part in defining an architectural space.

In houses with large dimensions, where there is a preponderance of the walls over the openings, color gains even more importance, so it is recommended that the chromatic compositions are selected to adjust to a unified whole, taking into consideration the environment that surrounds the architectural work.

LAS TEXTURAS, EL COLOR Y LA LUZ permiten apreciar las características tridimensionales del espacio y son componentes fundamentales en la definición de los espacios arquitectónicos.

En aquellas casas de fuertes volúmenes, con preponderancia de los muros sobre los vanos, el color adquiere aún mayor importancia, por lo que es recomendable ajustar las composiciones cromáticas que se elijan a un todo unificado, considerando también el medio ambiente que rodea a la obra arquitectónica.

LES TEXTURES, LES COULEURS ET LA LUMIERE permettent d'apprécier les caractéristiques tridimensionnelles de l'espace et elles sont des composantes fondamentales dans la définition des espaces architectoniques.

Dans les maisons aux forts volumes, où dominent les murs sur les embrasures, la couleur acquiert encore plus d'importance. Il est donc conseillé d'ajuster les compositions chromatiques choisies à un tout unifié, et de prendre également en compte l'environnement autour de l'œuvre architectonique.

exteriors
exteriores
extérieurs
außen

DIE TEXTUREN, DIE FARBE UND DAS LICHT erlauben die Würdigung von den dreidimensionalen Merkmalen des Raumes und sie sind wesentliche Bestandteile in der Definition der architektonischen Räume.

In jenen Häusern großer Dimensionen, mit Überwiegen der Mauern auf den Räumen, die Farbe erwirbt noch größere Wichtigkeit, wegen dieses, es ist ratsam, die gewählten chromatischen Zusammenstellungen zu einem vereintem Ganzen einzustellen, auch die Umgebung zu betrachten, die der architektonischen Arbeit umgibt.

Color and paint are two different things and it is convenient to take both into consideration when making the chromatic selection for a house. All construction materials have a natural color; there are stones and wood with different tones, as well as a wide range of reflective surfaces and colors of adobe, bricks, aluminum and iron, to name just a few. Resorting to the natural colors of construction materials can be highly beneficial for the ambiance generated in a space.

Color y pintura son dos cosas distintas y conviene tomar en consideración ambas al momento de realizar la selección cromática de una casa. Todos los materiales de construcción poseen un color natural; hay piedras y maderas de distintas tonalidades, así como extensas gamas de brillos y colores de adobes, ladrillos, aluminios y hierros, por nombrar solamente algunos. Puede resultar de gran beneficio para el ambiente que se genere en un espacio el auxiliarse de los colores de los materiales de construcción.

Couleur et peinture sont deux choses distinctes et il convient de les prendre toutes deux en compte au moment de procéder à la sélection chromatique d'une maison. Tous les matériaux de construction possèdent une couleur naturelle; il y a des pierres et des bois de tonalités différentes, ainsi qu'un grand nombre de gammes de brillants et de couleurs de brique crue, de brique, d'aluminium et de fer, pour n'en nommer seulement que quelques-uns. Utiliser les couleurs des matériaux de construction peut être très bénéfique pour le cadre créé dans un espace donné.

Farbe und Anstrich sind zwei verschiedene Sachen und um beide zu betrachten es ist wichtig, um die chromatische Auswahl eines Hauses zu realisieren. Alle Materialien für Konstruktion haben eine natürliche Farbe; es gibt Steine und Holz verschiedenartiger Tonalitäten, sowie umfangreiche Vielfalten von Glanz und Farben von Adobe, Backsteinen, Aluminium und Eisen, unter anderen. In einem Raum die Farhen der Materialien für Konstruktion zu erzeugen kann wohltuend für die Atmosphäre sein.

Typically, the colors used on the exterior of a house declare the individual identity of its residents and are related to the environs where the house is located. Colors inspired by those found in nature, especially those related to earth –ochre, red, yellow, terra cotta– combined with the greens in the surrounding vegetation, give a warm and cozy atmosphere to the architecture. The framing of window openings with colors that contrast and the use of woods with rustic treatment contribute to enhance said effect.

Por lo común, los colores utilizados en los exteriores de una casa expresan la identidad individual de sus habitantes y se relacionan con el entorno en donde se inserta la vivienda. Los colores inspirados en aquellos que se encuentran en la naturaleza, especialmente los relacionados con la tierra –ocre, rojo, amarillo, terracota–, combinados con los verdes de la vegetación circundante, le otorgan a la arquitectura una cálida y acogedora atmósfera. El enmarcado de los vanos de las ventanas con colores contrastantes y el empleo de maderas con tratamientos rústicos contribuyen a incrementar dicho efecto.

En général, les couleurs utilisées dans les extérieurs d'une maison reflètent l'identité individuelle de ses habitants et sont liées à l'environnement où se trouve le logement. Les couleurs inspirées de celles qu'on trouve dans la nature, en particulier celles qui sont liées à la terre, –ocre, rouge, jaune, terre cuite–, combinées aux verts de la végétation environnante, confèrent à l'architecture une atmosphère chaleureuse et accueillante. L'encadrement des embrasures des fenêtres par des couleurs contrastantes et l'emploi de bois aux traitements rustiques contribuent à accroître cet effet.

Im allgemeinen benutzten die Farben im Äußere eines Hauses, drücken die einzelne Identität ihrer Bewohner aus, und beeinflussen die Umgebung des Hauses. Die Farben inspirierten durch die Natur, besonders fügten die Farben mit der Erde zusammen –Ocker, rot, gelb, terracotta–, wenn diese mit dem Grün der umliegenden Vegetation kombiniert werden, sie geben zur Architektur eine warme und freundliche Atmosphäre. Der Fenster Rahmen mit gegensätzlichen Farben und der Anstellung von Holz mit ländlicher Stil zunehmen diese Wirkung.

To select the color of the walls and ceilings of a house it is convenient to take into consideration the temperature, sun and air conditions of the place. When the weather is warm it is preferable to use light colors on the exterior surfaces for the purpose of reducing heat, because, if dark tones are used, it will increase considerably.

Para la selección del color de muros y techos de una casa es conveniente considerar las condiciones de temperatura, sol y aire del lugar. Cuando el clima es cálido es preferible utilizar colores claros en las superficies exteriores con la finalidad de disminuir la ganancia de calor, pues, si se recurre a tonos oscuros ésta aumentará considerablemente.

Pour la sélection de la couleur des murs et des toits
d'une maison, il est nécessaire de prendre en compte les
conditions de température, d'ensoleillement et d'air du lieu.
Quand le climat est chaud, l'emploi de couleurs claires
sur les surfaces extérieures est préférable afin de diminuer
l'absorption de chaleur, car si l'on utilise des tons sombres,
celle-ci sera considérablement accrue.

Für die Auswahl der Farbe von Mauern und Dächern eines
Hauses ist es zweckmäßig, die Zustände von Temperatur,
Sonne und Luft der Stelle zu betrachten. wenn ist das Klima
warm, es ist besser, klare Farben in den externen Oberflächen
zu benutzen, um den Hitzegewinn zu verringern; weil die
Verwendung dunkler Tonalitäten zunehmen es beachtlich.

The contrast between the colors used on the facades, or between these and the natural environment, helps to generate effects of closeness and distance, creating a dynamic among the different architectural levels.

Los contrastes entre los colores usados en las fachadas, o entre éstos y el entorno natural, ayudan a generar percepciones de cercanía y lejanía, creando una dinámica entre los distintos planos arquitectónicos.

Les contrastes entre les couleurs utilisées sur les façades, ou entre les couleurs et l'environnement, contribuent à générer des perceptions de proximité et d'éloignement, et créent ainsi une dynamique au sein des divers plans architectoniques.

Die Kontraste zwischen den Farben, die in den Fassaden benutzt werden, oder zwischen diesen und der natürlichen Umgebung erzeugen Wahrnehmungen von Nähe und Entfernung und kreieren ein Dynamisch zwischen den verschiedenartigen architektonischen Räumen.

Selecting a strong color or a neutral one declares the introverted or outgoing personality of the building.

La selección de un color fuerte o de uno neutro expresa el carácter introvertido o extrovertido de la construcción.

Le choix d'une couleur forte ou neutre reflète le caractère introverti ou extraverti d'un bâtiment.

Die Auswahl von einer intensiven oder neutralen Farbe drücken den introvertierten oder extravertierten Charakter der Konstruktion aus.

The colors of the façades, whether intense or neutral, contrast in different degrees with those in nature, marking a greater or smaller presence of the house in the landscape.

Los colores de las fachadas, ya sean intensos o neutros, contrastan en diversos grados con los de la naturaleza, marcando una mayor o menor presencia de la casa en el paisaje.

Les couleurs des façades, qu'elles soient intenses ou neutres, contrastent de diverses façons avec celles de la nature, et donnent ainsi une présence, plus ou moins marquée, à la maison au sein du paysage.

Die Farben der Fassaden, intensiv oder neutral, stellen mit den Farben der Natur mannigfaltig gegenüber, und kreieren eine größere oder kleinere Anwesenheit des Hauses in der Landschaft.

In architectural works, the relationship between shape and color, on one side, and between the openings and the walls, on the other, are factors that determine the design. While the color of the walls distinguishes a house, their changing tones due to the effect of light throughout the day, together with shade, reflections and transparencies caused by empty spaces, as well as the nocturnal lighting that bursts across them, create, both during the day and during the night, a dynamic play of colors that multiplies the spatial interest of its exteriors.

En las obras arquitectónicas la relación entre forma y color, por una parte, y entre los vanos y los muros, por la otra, son factores determinantes del diseño. Mientras que el color de los muros distingue a una casa, las tonalidades cambiantes que éstos tienen por efecto de la luz a lo largo del día, aunadas a las sombras, reflejos y transparencias ocasionadas por los vacíos, así como a la iluminación nocturna que se desborda por ellos, crean, tanto de día como de noche, un juego dinámico de colores que multiplica el interés espacial de sus exteriores.

Dans les œuvres architectoniques, le rapport entre forme et couleur, d'une part, et entre les embrasures et les murs, d'autre part, sont des facteurs déterminants du plan et design. Tandis que la couleur des murs distingue une maison, les tonalités changeantes que ceux-ci acquièrent du fait des changements de luminosité durant la journée, de l'ombre, des reflets et de la transparence provoquée par les vides, et de l'éclairage nocturne qui les inonde, créent, de jour comme de nuit, un jeu dynamique de couleurs qui multiplie l'intérêt spatial des extérieurs d'une maison.

In den architektonischen Arbeiten, die Verbindung zwischen Form und Farbe, und die Verbindung zwischen den Räumen und den Mauern sind entscheidende Faktoren des Design. Während die Farbe der Mauern ein Haus unterscheidet, die verändernd Tonalitäten wegen der Wirkung des Lichtes während des Tages, sowie die Schatten, Spiegelungen und Transparenzen verursachten durch die Leere und die Nachtillumination, kreieren im Tag und Nacht ein Farbenkontrast, welcher vervielfacht das Rauminteresse ihrer Äußere.

Paint allows for transforming the natural appearance of materials, their shine, their texture and their color; nevertheless, before making any decision it is necessary to study and test the effect of light on the changes. Whether to use a material that maintains its original appearance or is modified depends only on the taste and personality of the occupants of a house.

La pintura permite transformar la apariencia natural de los materiales, su brillo, su textura y su color; no obstante, antes de tomar cualquier decisión es necesario estudiar y ensayar la acción que tendrá la luz sobre los cambios. Si un material es expuesto con su apariencia original o si esta última es modificada, en realidad sólo depende del gusto y la personalidad de los usuarios de una casa.

La peinture permet de transformer l'apparence naturelle,
le brillant, la texture et la couleur des matériaux; néanmoins,
avant de prendre quelque décision que ce soit, il est
nécessaire d'étudier et de tester l'action que la lumière aura
sur ces changements. En réalité, qu'un matériel soit exposé
dans son apparence originale, ou si celle-ci est modifiée,
dépend uniquement des goûts et de la personnalité des
usagers d'une maison.

Das Gemälde erlaubt die Verwandlung vom natürlichen
Aussehen der Materialien, sowie ihr Glanz, ihre Textur und ihre
Farbe; trotzdem ist es notwendig die Analyse und die Prüfung
von der Handlung, die das Licht die Änderungen anhaben
wird, vor irgendeiner Entscheidung. Wenn ein Material
mit seinem originalen Aussehen freigelegt wird, oder dies
wird modifiziert, in Wirklichkeit hängt es nur vom Gusto und
Persönlichkeit von den Benutzern eines Hauses ab.

THE COLOR assigned to a living room, or any other living space, influences the feeling that the space transmits and it is part of its customization. When colors derived from red and yellow are applied, there is a feeling of warmth, while the use of colors which come from blue helps to create a colder atmosphere. Likewise, discreet colors may suggest peace and strong colors evoke the impression of being in juvenile and joyous ambiances. The balance between colors and weather is useful for generating comfortable spaces.

EL COLOR que se de a una sala, o a cualquier otro espacio de estar, influye en la sensación que se transmita del espacio y es parte de su personalización. Cuando se aplican colores derivados del rojo y del amarillo se obtiene una sensación de calidez, mientras que el uso de colores que provienen del azul ayuda a conformar atmósferas más frías.

De igual modo, los colores discretos pueden sugerir serenidad y los fuertes evocar impresiones de estar en ambientes juveniles y alegres. El equilibrio entre colores y clima es útil para generar espacios confortables.

LA COULEUR donnée à une salle de séjour, ou à un autre espace de séjour, influe sur l'impression qu'on transmet de l'espace et elle est partie intégrante de sa personnalisation. Quand on applique des couleurs dérivées du rouge et du jaune, on obtient une sensation de chaleur, tandis que l'emploi de couleurs dérivées du bleu contribue à conformer des atmosphères plus froides. De même, les couleurs discrètes peuvent suggérer sérénité et les couleurs fortes donner l'impression d'être dans des ambiances jeunes et joyeuses. L'équilibre entre les couleurs et le climat est utile pour créer des espaces confortables.

DIE FARBE erhielt in einem Zimmer, oder in irgendeinem anderen Raum, beeinflußt in der Sensation, die der Raum übersendet, und es ist Teil seines Persönlichmachen. Wenn rötliche und gelbe Farben benutzt werden, eine Sensation von Wärme wird erhalten, und die Verwendung blauer Farben kreiert kältere Atmosphären. Die diskreten Farben verursachen Gelassenheit und die starken rufen jugendliche und fröhliche Atmosphären hervor. Das Gleichgewicht zwischen Farben und Klima ist nützlich, um bequeme Räume zu erzeugen.

living rooms
salas
salons
wohnzimmer

There is a great variety of woods with warm tones that may be used for covering large surfaces like floors, ceilings or walls and which, also, when combined with furniture and other layers in discreet colors, contribute to creating clean and elegant ambiances. These atmospheres are markedly enhanced when they come in contact both with natural lighting from outside, as well as different sources of light that have been designed to provide comfort to the room when the evening falls and at night.

Hay gran variedad de maderas de tonalidades cálidas que se pueden usar como recubrimientos en grandes superficies, ya sea en pisos, techos o muros y que, además, cuando son combinadas con muebles y otros planos en colores discretos cooperan a crear ambientes limpios y elegantes. Estas atmósferas se enriquecen notablemente cuando entran en contacto tanto con la iluminación natural proveniente del exterior, como con aquélla que ha sido planeada para brindar confort al espacio al caer la tarde y por la noche, y que procede de diversos tipos de luminarios.

Il y a une grande variété de bois aux tonalités chaudes qui peuvent être utilisés comme revêtements de grandes surfaces, que ce soit des sols, des toits ou des murs, et qui, combinés à des meubles et à d'autres plans de couleurs discrètes, contribuent à créer des cadres propres et élégants. Ces atmosphères s'enrichissent notablement au contact de l'éclairage naturel provenant de l'extérieur ainsi que de celui qui a été planifié pour rendre l'espace confortable, à la tombée du jour et la nuit, qui provient de divers types de luminaires.

Es gibt große Vielfalt von Holz mit warmen Tonalitäten, daß kann als das Decken in großen Oberflächen benutzt werden, wie in Böden, Dächern oder Mauern, auch, wenn sie mit Möbel und anderen Oberflächen mit diskreten Farben kombiniert werden, macht ein sauber und elegant Umgebungs. Diese Atmosphären anreichern mit der natürlichen Illumination des Äußere auffallend, und bieten Bequemlichkeit zum Raum am Nachmittag sowie in der Nacht an, wegen der verschiedenartigen Arten von Illuminierungen.

Through isolated objects, which should not weigh too much on the interior design of a living room, it is possible to give a touch of color to spaces where a monochromatic palette of colors has been selected. This way, pillows, small couches, ornamental devices, paintings, lampshades and even a plant can become focal points.

A través de objetos aislados, que no pesen mucho en el interiorismo de una sala, es posible dar un toque de color a espacios en los que se ha seleccionado una paleta de colores monocromática. De este modo, cojines, pequeños sillones, objetos de ornamentación, cuadros, las pantallas de las lámparas de mesa y hasta alguna planta pueden convertirse en puntos focales.

Au travers d'objets isolés, qui ne pèsent pas trop dans l'intériorité d'une salle de séjour, on peut donner une touche de couleur à des espaces où on a choisi une palette de couleurs monochromatique. De cette façon, les coussins, les petits fauteuils, les objets décoratifs, les tableaux, les écrans des lampes, et même une plante, peuvent devenir des points focaux.

Es ist möglich, daß die Räume mit monochromen Tonalitäten mehr Farbe durch isolierte Gegenstände bekommen, daß kombiniert mit dem Interieur eines Zimmers. Zum Beispiel, Polster, kleine Lehnstühle, Gegenstände von Verzierung, Bilder, die Lampenschirme und irgendeine Pflanze können Brennpunkte werden.

When there is a predominance of light tones in the environment, one can add a great touch of color to the space by incorporating large-format paintings, which also open the possibility of transforming the walls into attractive art galleries. Another option is to apply a color, with enough strength and character, over one of the walls, inciting its viewing and helping to break up the monotony of the space. Said solution also helps for headings, supports, and other elements.

Cuando en los ambientes existe la predominancia de tonos claros se puede agregar una gran nota de color al espacio a través de la incorporación de cuadros de grandes formatos, que además abren la posibilidad de convertir a los muros en atractivas galerías de arte. Otra opción es la de aplicar un color, que tenga suficiente fuerza y carácter, sobre alguna de las paredes, incitando el apoyo de la vista sobre ella y cooperando a romper con la monotonía del espacio. Esta última solución ayuda también a configurar cabeceras, respaldos, entre otros elementos.

Lorsque le cadre est dominé par des tons clairs, on peut ajouter une grande note de couleur à l'espace grâce à l'incorporation de tableaux de grands formats qui permettent que les murs deviennent ainsi d'attrayantes galeries d'art. Une autre option consiste à appliquer une couleur, qui ait la force et le caractère suffisants, sur un des murs, afin d'attirer l'attention du regard et de rompre la monotonie de l'espace. Cette dernière solution contribue aussi à configurer des chevets et des dossiers, entre autres éléments.

Wenn die Vorherrschaft klarer Farben in den Atmosphären existiert, man kann mehr Farbe zum Raum durch die Einverleibung großer Bilder hinzufügen, es gibt auch die Möglichkeit, die Mauern in attraktive Kunstgalerien umzugestalten. Noch eine Möglichkeit ist die Anwendung einer Farbe, mit genug Laut und Charakter auf irgendeiner Mauer, um anzuziehen und die Eintönigkeit des Raumes zu brechen. Diese Lösung gestaltet Kopfbretter, Rückenstützen, unter anderen Elementen auch.

Sometimes color serves to differentiate and delimit the interior spaces of a house; sometimes it is used to finish off a space or to frame it, or to accentuate the shape of its dimensions.

A veces el color sirve para diferenciar y delimitar los espacios interiores de una casa; otras es utilizado para rematar un espacio o para encuadrarlo, o bien para acentuar la forma de sus volúmenes.

Parfois, la couleur sert à différencier et délimiter les espaces intérieurs d'une maison; et d'autres fois, la couleur est utilisée pour parachever un espace ou pour l'encadrer, ou bien encore pour accentuer la forme de ses volumes.

Manchmal, die Farbe unterscheidet und definiert die innenen Räume eines Hauses; und anderes Mal ergänzt oder rahmt einen Raum, oder akzentuieren die Form ihrer Dimensionen auch.

The impression of depth in a place may be modified by the brightness and luminosity of the colors. When the hallways are long and narrow, it is convenient to use bright colors at the end to create the feeling of closeness, and if they are short and wide it is preferable to resort to strong and dull colors to generate the feeling of greater distance.

Cuando los pasillos son largos y angostos conviene usar en su fondo colores luminosos para crear sensación de cercanía, mientras que si son cortos y anchos es preferible recurrir a colores fuertes y menos luminosos para provocar una sensación de mayor lejanía.

Lorsque les couloirs sont longs et étroits, il convient d'utiliser, dans leur fond, des couleurs lumineuses pour créer une impression de proximité. S'ils sont, au contraire, courts et larges, il est préférable de recourir à des couleurs fortes et moins lumineuses pour donner une impression de plus grande distance.

Wenn sind die Korridore lang und verengen, es ist ratsam, in ihren unterst leuchtenden Farben zu benutzen, um Nähesensation zu kreieren; wenn sind kurz und weit, es ist vorzuziehend, starke und leuchtende Farben zu benutzen, um eine Sensation von mehr Fntfernung zu verursachen. Het gebruikt niet de drukken in zijn samenstellingen, gebruikt eerder vlotte textiel.

The living room is a space that may be arranged in very different ways and in which the color project is associated with other links and considerations for the design: formality, warmth, simplicity, sobriety, liveliness, elegance…; for any of these, the layout should not be too complicated, because, due to its natural function, this space develops its own visual diversity. The use of smooth and clear colors for the furniture and surfaces, combined with the transparencies and the sober accessory lines, favors a clean ambiance and accentuates the effect of order.

La sala es un espacio que se puede resolver de muy distintos modos y en el que el proyecto del color se asocia a otros vínculos y consideraciones del diseño: formalidad, calidad, sencillez, sobriedad, vitalidad, elegancia…; en cualquiera de los casos, el planteamiento no debe ser muy complicado, pues, por su función natural, este espacio desarrolla su propia pluralidad visual. El uso de colores tenues y claros en mobiliario y en superficies, aunado a las transparencias y a los accesorios de líneas sobrias, favorece los ambientes de limpieza y acentúa el efecto de orden.

La salle de séjour est un espace qu'on peut arranger de façons très différentes et où le projet de couleur s'associe à d'autres liens et considérations du plan et design: la formalité, la qualité, la simplicité, la sobriété, la vitalité, l'élégance... Quel que soit le cas, le projet ne doit pas être trop compliqué, car du fait de sa fonction naturelle, cet espace développe sa propre pluralité visuelle. L'utilisation de couleurs pâles et claires sur un mobilier et des surfaces, ainsi que la transparence et les accessoires aux lignes sobres, favorise un cadre de propreté et accentue l'impression d'ordre.

Das Wohnzimmer ist ein Raum mit vielen Möglichkeiten, wo das Projekt der Farbe zu anderen Begriffen und Überlegungen des Designs verbunden wird: Förmlichkeit, Qualität, Einfachheit, Nüchternheit, Energie, Eleganz...; jedenfalls sollte die Vorstellung nicht sehr kompliziert sein, wegen seiner natürlichen Funktion entwickelt dieser Raum seine eigene visuelle Mehrheit. Die Verwendung delikater und klarer Farben in Möbel und Oberflächen, sowie die Transparenzen und die feinen Zubehöre, begünstigen die Reinigenatmosphären, und akzentuieren die Dekorationwirkung.

Colors may be displayed fully and without alteration or by controlling their degree of saturation by mixing them with white, black or gray. The chromatic intensity of the color affects the perception of the space; when resorting to intense colors, with the highest purity of their hue, one has to be careful to combine them with other walls with neutral colors or to have window and door openings to avoid a feeling of less space.

Los colores pueden ser expuestos en todo su potencial y sin alteraciones o controlando su grado de saturación a través de su mezcla con blanco, negro o gris. La intensidad cromática del color afecta la percepción que se tiene del espacio; cuando se recurre a colores intensos, con la más alta pureza de su tinte, hay que cuidar que sean combinados con otros muros en colores neutros o bien que se cuente con vanos de puertas y ventanas para evitar la sensación de menor amplitud del espacio.

Les couleurs peuvent être exposées dans tout leur potentiel et sans altérations, ou bien en contrôlant leur degré de saturation à travers leur mélange avec du blanc, du noir ou du gris. L'intensité chromatique de la couleur affecte la perception que l'on a de l'espace; lorsque l'on a recours à des couleurs intenses, d'une teinte de la plus haute pureté, il faut veiller à ce que celles-ci soient assorties à d'autres murs de couleurs neutres, ou bien à ce qu'on puisse disposer d'embrasures de portes et de fenêtres pour éviter l'impression de moindre ampleur de l'espace.

Die Farben können in all ihrem Potential freigelegt werden und ohne Änderungen, oder ihre Tränkung kann kontrolliert werden, durch seine Mischung mit weißem, schwarz oder grau. Die chromatische Intensität der Farbe beeinflußt die Wahrnehmung des Raumes; wenn wir intensive Farben benutzen, mit der höchsten Reinheit in ihrem Farbton, diese sollten mit anderen Mauern in Neutrumfarben kombiniert werden oder Räume mit Türen und Fenstern zu haben, um die Sensatic von weniger Weite zu vermeiden.

dining rooms
comedores
salles à manger
eßzimmer

FOR THE PURPOSE OF ACHIEVING A HARMONIC AMBIANCE in the dining areas it is better to limit the outlet of color and texture. White or beige tones on walls and tapestries, combined with the dark, copper and red tones of furniture and accessories, contribute to create bold, pure and elegant designs that also bring out the three-dimensional nature of the space.

The use of these pigments alludes to calm atmospheres and may be useful for highlighting, by way of contrast, the colors of food and beverages.

CON EL OBJETO DE LOGRAR UN CLIMA ARMÓNICO en los espacios destinados al comedor es conveniente que la descarga de colores y texturas sea limitada. Los tonos blancos o beiges en paredes y tapicerías, combinados con los pardos, cobrizos y rojizos del mobiliario y los accesorios contribuyen a formar diseños audaces, puros y elegantes que, además, resaltan la tridimensionalidad del espacio.

El uso de estos pigmentos alude a atmósferas de tranquilidad y pueden resultar de gran utilidad para hacer sobresalir, por contraste, los colores de los propios alimentos y bebidas.

AFIN D'OBTENIR UN CLIMAT HARMONIEUX au sein des espaces destinés à la salle à manger, il convient que l'utilisation des couleurs et textures soit mesurée. Les tons blancs ou beiges sur les murs et les tapisseries, assortis aux bruns, aux cuivrés et rougeâtres du mobilier et des accessoires, contribuent à former des plans et designs audacieux, purs et élégants qui, en plus, mettent en valeur la tridimensionnalité de l'espace.

L'emploi de ces pigments correspond à des atmosphères paisibles et peuvent être de grande utilité pour faire ressortir, par effet de contraste, les couleurs des aliments et des boissons.

ES IST RATSAM DIE BEGRENZT Begleichung von Farben und Texturen, um ein harmonisches Klima in den Eßzimmern zu erreichen. Die weißen oder beigen Tonalitäten in Mauern und Gobelins, kombiniert mit braun, kupferartig und rötlich vom Möbel und Zubehören kreieren dreiste, reine und vornehme Designs, außer, sie stehen dem dreidimensionalen Raum heraus.

Die Verwendung dieser Pigmente deutet Ruheatmosphären hin, und sie können sehr nützlich sein, um die Farben von den Essen und Getränken herauszustehen.

Red and brown colors in dining rooms create sociable environments and stimulate appetite; but it is recommended that they be used discreetly, since they can be overwhelming if used in excess.

Los tonos rojos, usados en forma discreta crean ambientes sociables y estimulan el apetito; utilizados en exceso pueden resultar abrumadores.

Les couleurs rouges et châtaines dans les salles à manger créent un cadre de sociabilité et stimulent l'appétit; utilisérs en excès, elles peuvent résulter oppressantes.

Die roten und braunen Farben in Eßzimmern kreieren gesellige Atmosphären und stimulieren den Appetit; aber es ist ratsam, sie diskret zu benutzen, weil in Überschuß sie überwältigen können.

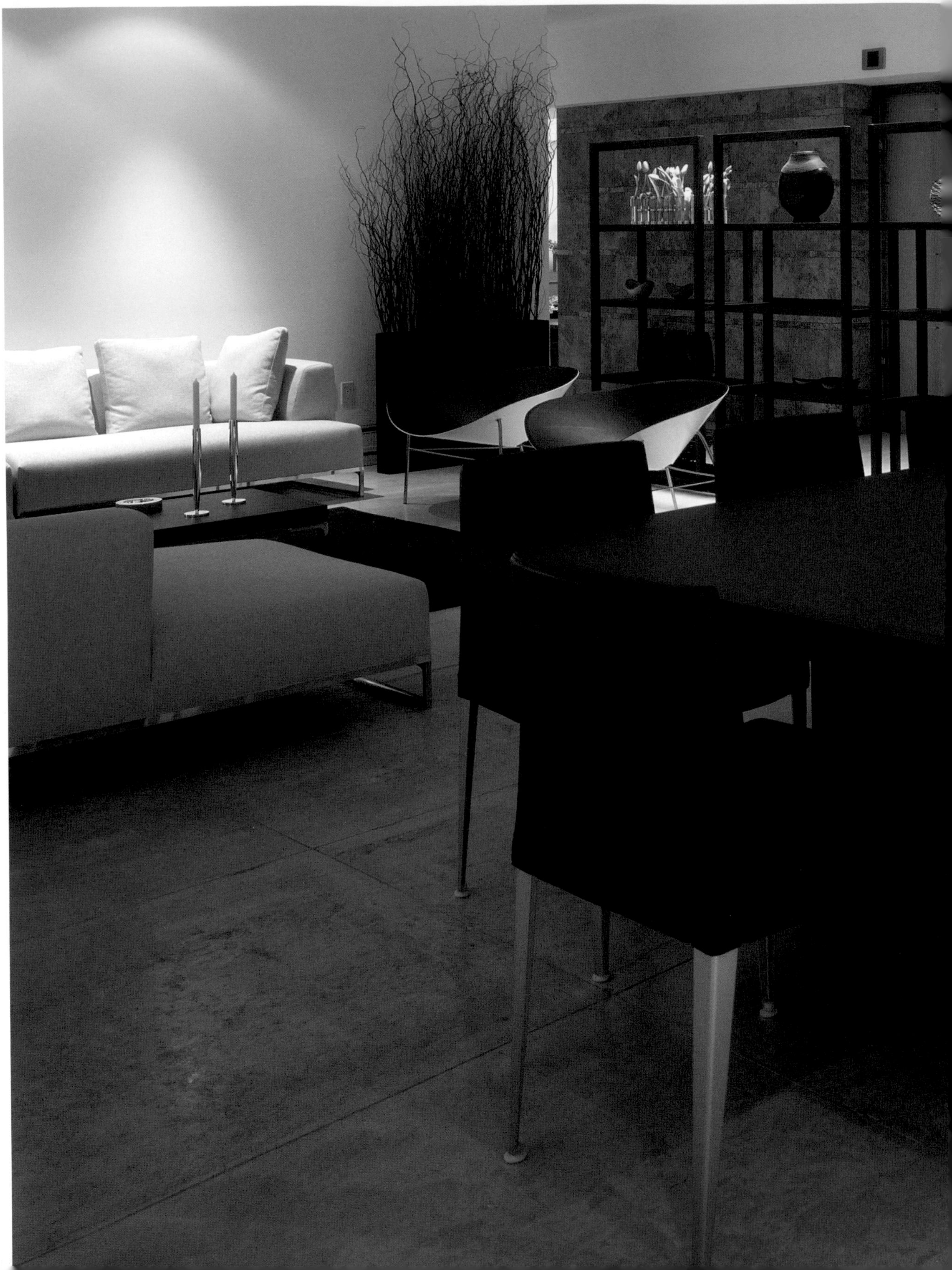

THE KITCHEN FURNITURE OPTIONS available on the market have allowed this space to gain great significance for design and for color to become a leading factor. Even though the chromatic choice of the kitchen is related to personal taste and the conditions of each space, it is recommended that the tone selected be considered, that its luminosity and reflections allow for maximum visibility when cooking, make cleaning easier and create hygienic spaces.

LAS OPCIONES DE MOBILIARIO DE COCINA que existen en el mercado han permitido que este espacio adquiera gran significado para el diseño y que el color se convierta en un factor protagónico. Aunque la selección cromática de la cocina tiene que ver con el gusto personal y con las condiciones de cada espacio, es recomendable considerar que el tono que se elija, su luminosidad y sus reflejos permitan la óptima visibilidad al preparar los alimentos, faciliten la limpieza y creen ambientes de higiene.

LES OPTIONS DE MOBILIER DE CUISINE qui existent sur le marché ont permis que cet espace acquière une grande signification pour le plan et design, et que la couleur devienne un facteur primordial. Bien que la sélection chromatique de la cuisine soit liée aux goûts personnels et aux conditions de chaque espace, il est conseillé de veiller à ce que la tonalité choisie, sa luminosité et ses reflets permettent une parfaite visibilité pour faire la cuisine, facilitent le nettoyage et créent un cadre hygiénique.

DIE KÜCHEN HABEN GROßE Wichtigkeit für das Design erworben, wegen der verschiedenartigen Optionen von Küchenmöbel im Markt, wo die Farbe ein sehr wichtiger Faktor ist. Obwohl die chromatische Auswahl der Küche hängt vom persönlichen Gusto und den Zuständen jedes Raumes ab, es ist ratsam, daß die Helligkeit und Highlight der Farbe die gute Sichtbarkeit in der Vorbereitung der Essen erlauben, erleichtern der Sauberkeit und kreieren hygienisch Umgebungs.

kitchens
cocinas
cuisines
küchen

Sometimes the color of the kitchen may be dominated by the color of its furniture, while other times it is defined by the colors on the walls.

Algunas veces el color de la cocina puede estar dominado por el propio color de sus muebles, mientras que en otras son los colores utilizados en muros los que lo definen.

Dans certains cas, la couleur de la cuisine peut être dominée par la propre couleur de ses meubles, tandis que dans d'autres, ce sont les couleurs des murs qui la définissent.

Manchmal wird die Farbe der Küche durch die Farbe seines Möbel dominiert, oder die Farben benutzten in Mauern.

baths baños salles de bains badezimmer

The colors used in the bathrooms may provide sensorial spaces; clear and cold colors evoke relaxation, amplitude, cleanliness and freshness; while the warm colors are spectacular and make up dynamic ambiances.

Los colores usados en baños pueden proporcionar ámbitos de sensación; los claros y fríos evocan relajación, amplitud, limpieza y frescor; mientras que los cálidos son espectaculares y componen ambientes dinámicos.

Les couleurs utilisées dans les salles de bains contribuent à créer un cadre d'émotion; les couleurs claires et froides évoquent la détente, l'ampleur, la propreté et la fraîcheur, tandis que les couleurs chaudes sont spectaculaires et conforment un cadre dynamique.

Die Farben in den Badezimmern kreieren Umgebungen von Sensation; die klaren und kalte Farben provozieren Entspannung, Weite, Sauberkeit und Kühle; während die warmen spektakulär sind, und setzen dynamische Atmosphären zusammen.

THE HARMONY that may be achieved through the use of simple geometric and linear shapes both from the design of the space, and from the furniture and accessories selected, is enriched when one resorts to color variations from a single palette, or black and white and in their different tones. Nevertheless, in some cases it is better to break the monotony of an atmosphere by introducing an element of vibrant color, or an object that stands out.

LA ARMONÍA que se puede lograr mediante el uso de formas geométricas simples y lineales tanto en el diseño del espacio como en el del mobiliario y accesorios de baño que se seleccionen, se enriquece al recurrir a paletas de colores provenientes de una misma gama o bien al blanco y al negro en sus distintos matices. No obstante, en algunos casos conviene romper con la monotonía de la atmósfera generada, a través de la introducción de algún elemento de color vivo o de algún objeto que sobresalga.

L'HARMONIE qu'on peut obtenir grâce à l'emploi de formes géométriques simples et linéaires, tant dans le plan et design de l'espace que dans celui du mobilier et des accessoires de bain choisis, s'enrichit si l'on a recours à des palettes de couleurs dérivées d'une même gamme, ou bien au blanc et au noir dans leurs diverses nuances. Dans certains cas, il convient, néanmoins, de rompre la monotonie de l'atmosphère générée par l'introduction d'un élément de couleur vive ou d'un objet qui ressorte.

DIE HARMONIE, die mittels der Verwendung einfacher und in gerader Linie geometrischer Formen im Design des Raumes erreicht werden kann, sowie im Möbel und Badezimmer-Zubehör, es anreichert wenn man Farben ähnlicher Tonalitäten benutzt, oder weiß und schwarz in ihren verschiedenartigen Schatten auch. Trotzdem manchmal ist besser, mit der Eintönigkeit der erzeugte Atmosphäre zu brechen, durch irgendein buntes Element oder auffälligen Gegenstand.

While the option of using discreet colors from the same palette on juxtaposed walls in bathrooms helps to create an ambience of cleanliness, elegance and aesthetic value, one can also choose from a palette of strong and contrasting colors that will give the space liveliness and warmth. In any case, it is recommended that the color chosen be related to the lighting quality of the space, because this is indispensable for avoiding the loss of the functionality of the space.

Si bien la opción de utilizar en las paredes yuxtapuestas de los baños colores en tonos discretos y provenientes de la misma gama coopera a crear ambientes de limpieza, elegancia y de alta calidad estética, también se puede optar por una paleta de colores fuertes y contrastados que le otorguen vitalidad y calidez al espacio. En cualquiera de los casos, es recomendable que el color que se elija esté relacionado con la calidad de iluminación del espacio, pues ésta es indispensable para que no se pierda la funcionalidad del mismo.

Même si l'emploi de couleurs de tons discrets et dérivés de la même gamme sur les murs juxtaposés des salles de bains contribue à créer un cadre propre, élégant et de grande qualité esthétique, on peut aussi opter pour une palette de couleurs fortes et contrastées qui donnent vitalité et chaleur à l'espace. Dans tous les cas, il est conseillé que la couleur choisie soit en accord avec la qualité de l'éclairage de l'espace, car celui-ci est essentiel afin que l'espace ne perde pas sa fonctionnalité.

Die Verwendung von Farben mit diskreten Lauten und von der gleichen Tonalität in den nebeneinandergestellt Mauern der Badezimmer kreiert Umgebungs von Sauberkeit, Eleganz und hoher ästhetischer Qualität, auch kann man starke und intensive Farben wählen, um Energie und Wärme im Raum zu kreieren. Jedenfalls ist es ratsam, eine Farbe in Verbindung mit der Qualität von Illumination des Raumes zu wählen, dies ist unentbehrlich, um seine Funktionalität nicht zu verlieren.

terraces
terrazas
terrasses
terrassen

EARTH TONES, which come from orange, red and yellow, are commonly suitable for applying on most terraces, because they generate a joyous ambiance, are warm and capture attention. In addition, these tones combine with the greens in nature and with the varied colors of flowers, helping to create interesting plays of contrast.

EL USO DE COLORES TÉRREOS, provenientes de naranjas, rojos y amarillos, generalmente es adecuado para aplicar en una buena parte de las terrazas, pues éstos generan un clima alegre, son cálidos y capturan la atención. Adicionalmente, estas tonalidades combinan con los verdes de la naturaleza y con los diversos coloridos de las flores, ayudando a la composición de juegos interesantes de contraste.

L'UTILISATION DE COULEURS TERREUSES, dérivées d'oranges, de rouges et de jaunes, est généralement adéquate pour les appliquer sur bonne partie des terrasses, car ce sont des couleurs chaudes qui créent un cadre gai et attirent l'attention. De plus, ces tonalités sont assorties aux verts de la nature et aux divers coloris des fleurs, ce qui contribue à la création de jeux de contraste intéressants.

DIE VERWENDUNG VON ORANGE, rot und gelb, gewöhnlich werden sie in den Terrassen benutzt, weil sie ein heitres Klima kreieren und sind warm und attraktiv. Diese Farben kombinieren mit dem Grün der Natur und mit den verschiedenartigen Färbungen der Blumen, dieser Weg sie kreieren eine interessante Dekoration.

The relationship of the color used for the spaces that connect inside and outside spaces must be carefully planned. To chose for the outside a palette of colors similar to that used in the inside strengthens harmony between the two spaces, creating subtle and relaxed atmospheres. When working under this scheme, it is recommended that the chromatic intensity be increased or decreased from one zone to another, using both paint as well as the pigments obtained from lighting effects, without forgetting the colors in vegetation and furniture.

La relación del uso del color entre los ambientes que conectan interiores con exteriores debe ser bien pensada. Elegir para los exteriores una paleta de colores similar a la utilizada en los interiores refuerza la armonía entre ambos espacios, creando atmósferas sutiles y relajadas. Cuando se trabaja bajo este esquema, es recomendable rebajar o aumentar la intensidad cromática de una zona a otra, recurriendo tanto a la pintura como a los pigmentos que se obtienen por efectos de la luz, sin perder de vista los colores de la vegetación y del mobiliario.

On doit bien penser le rapport de couleurs des lieux qui lient les intérieurs aux extérieurs. Choisir, pour les extérieurs, une palette de couleurs semblable à celle utilisée pour les intérieurs renforce l'harmonie entre ces deux espaces et crée ainsi des atmosphères subtiles et détendues. Quand on travaille en suivant ce schéma, il est conseillé de diminuer ou d'accroître l'intensité chromatique d'un site à un autre, en recourant tant à la peinture qu'aux pigments obtenus par les effets de la lumière, sans perdre de vue les couleurs de la végétation et du mobilier.

Die Verbindung zwischen den Farben, die das Interieur mit das Exterieur verbinden, sollte gut gedacht werden. wenn man wählt ähnliche Farben im Interieur und Exterieur, dies verstärkt die Harmonie zwischen beiden Räumen, und macht feine und entspannte Atmosphären. Wenn man unter diesem Plan arbeitet, es ist ratsam, zu reduzieren oder zu vergrößern die chromatische Intensität von einem Gebiet zu ein andere, das Gemälde zu betrachten sowie die Pigmente von den Wirkungen des Lichtes, ohne der Farben der Vegetation und Möbel zu verlieren.

light
luz
lumière
licht

exteriors   exteriores   extérieurs   außen

IT IS CLEAR that the cycles of life depend essentially on their relationship with the qualities and properties of light. Likewise, architecture, as a manifestation of life, has a similar connection. Life and architecture are not conceivable without the existence of light, because it gives presence and meaning to the space.

With the Modern Movement, the study of the close relationship between space and light was intensified, and the component of time was added, because it is indispensable for living the spaces.

EVIDENTEMENTE, los ciclos de la vida dependen esencialmente de su relación con las bondades y propiedades de la luz. De igual manera, la arquitectura, como manifestación de la vida, mantiene un vínculo semejante. Vida y arquitectura no son concebibles sin la existencia de la luz, pues es ésta la que le da presencia y sentido al espacio.

Con el Movimiento Moderno se intensificó el estudio de la relación estrecha entre espacio y luz, componentes a los que se les sumó el tiempo, como otro elemento importante que califica el modo de vivir los espacios.

IL EST EVIDENT que les cycles de la vie dépendent essentiellement de leur relation avec les qualités et les propriétés de la lumière. De même, l'architecture, en tant que manifestation de la vie, maintient un rapport similaire. On ne peut concevoir la vie et l'architecture sans l'existence de la lumière, vu que c'est elle qui donne une présence et un sens à l'espace.

Avec le Mouvement Moderne, l'étude du rapport étroit entre l'espace et la lumière s'est intensifiée. A ces éléments, s'est joint le temps puisque celui-ci est indispensable pour vivre les espaces.

AUGENSCHEINLICH, die Zyklen des Leben hängen im Grunde von seiner Verbindung mit der Gutartigkeit und Eigenschaften des Lichtes ab. In einem gleichen Weg, als Manifestation des Lebens, die Architektur behält eine ähnliche Verbindung bei. Leben und Architektur sind nicht vorstellbar ohne die Existenz des Lichtes, weil dies das Wesentliche und den Sinn dem Raum gibt.

Mit der Modernen Bewegung wurde das Studium der Verbindung zwischen Raum und Licht intensiviert, sehr wichtige Bestandteile, unentbehrlich um die Räume zu leben.

TO MAKE THE BEST POSSIBLE DESIGN of a house, it is necessary to become more aware, among other things, of the way that light is handled, as well as to take into consideration the qualities and tints of the daylight or when the architecture is marked by artificial lighting at night. With the proper management of light, it becomes possible to define, bring out and prioritize the dimensions of the elements that make up a house, as well as accent its architectural details and the textures of the materials used during its construction.

PARA REALIZAR EL MEJOR DISEÑO posible de una casa es necesario sensibilizarse, entre otras cosas, con el manejo de la luz, así como tomar en cuenta las diferencias de calidades y matices que existen ante la presencia de la luz del día o cuando la arquitectura está calificada por la iluminación artificial por las noches. Con el correcto manejo de la luz se hace posible definir, resaltar y jerarquizar la volumetría de los componentes que constituyen una casa, así como acentuar sus detalles constructivos y las texturas de los materiales que se emplean durante su construcción.

POUR REALISER LE MEILLEUR PLAN ET DESIGN possible d'une maison, il est nécessaire de se sensibiliser, entre autres, au maniement de la lumière et aussi de prendre en compte les différences de qualités et de nuances qui existent en présence de la lumière du jour ou lorsque, la nuit, l'architecture est baignée par l'éclairage artificiel. Si le maniement de la lumière est correct, il devient alors possible de définir, mettre en valeur et hiérarchiser la volumétrie des éléments d'une maison, et également d'accentuer ses détails constructifs et les textures des matériaux qui s'emploient durant sa construction.

UM DAS BESTEN DESIGN EINES HAUSES auszuführen es ist notwendig, mit der Verwendung des Lichtes sensibilisiert zu werden, unter anderen Dingen, sowie die Unterschiede von Qualitäten und Schatten zu erwägen, welche existieren bei der Gegenwart vom Licht des Tages oder, wenn die Architektur durch die künstliche Illumination bei Nächten qualifiziert wird. Mit dem geeigneten Licht ist es möglich, die Dimensionen von den Bestandteilen eines Hauses zu definieren, zu erausstehen und zu sortieren, sowie die Betonung der konstruktiven tails und der Texturen der Materialien, welche werden während Konstruktion benutzt.

The multiplication of the images and the unfolding of the space through the reflections made possible by the light are important design resources worth experimenting with.

La multiplicación de las imágenes y el desdoblamiento de los espacios a través de los reflejos que posibilita la luz, son recursos importantes de diseño que vale la pena experimentar.

La multiplication des images et le dédoublement des espaces, grâce aux reflets que permet la lumière, sont des ressources importantes du plan et design qui valent la peine d'être expérimentées.

Die Multiplikation der Bilder und die Erweiterung der Räumen durch die Highlights sind wichtige Designressourcen, die lohnend zu Erfahrung sind.

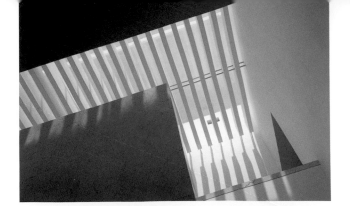

It is not possible to conceive of light without its counterpart, shadow. In the project of the exterior dimensions of a house, or of its patios, both elements have presence. When light is wisely complemented by the proper design of the floors and furniture, combined with the effects produced by the trees and bushes of the surrounding landscape, one can compose a symphony of lights and shadows that grant the architectural work a calm and dynamic personality which is always strongly expressive.

No es posible concebir la luz sin su contraparte, la sombra. En el proyecto de la volumetría exterior de una casa, o de los patios con los que ésta cuente, ambos elementos están presentes. Cuando la luz está sabiamente complementada por el diseño adecuado de los pisos y del mobiliario, aunada a los efectos producidos por los árboles y arbustos del paisaje circundante, se puede llegar a conformar una sinfonía de luces y sombras que le otorgan a la obra arquitectónica un carácter sereno o dinámico, pero siempre fuertemente expresivo.

On ne peut concevoir la lumière sans sa contrepartie, l´ombre. Dans le projet de la volumétrie extérieure d'une maison, ou des cours dont elle dispose, les deux éléments sont présents. Quand la lumière est savamment complétée par le plan et design adéquat des étages et du mobilier, et alliée aux effets produits par les arbres et les arbustes du paysage environnant, on parvient à conformer une symphonie d'ombres et de lumières qui donnent à l'œuvre architectonique un caractère serein ou dynamique, mais toujours fortement expressif.

Es ist nicht möglich, das Licht ohne sein Gegenstück auszudenken, der Schatten. Im dimensionalen Projekt eines Hauses, oder seiner Patios, beide Elemente sind anwesend. Wenn das Licht vom geeigneten Design der Böden und Möbel weise ergänzt wird, verbunden mit den Wirkungen, die durch die Bäume und Büsche der umliegenden Landschaft produziert werden, eine Symphonie von Lichtern und Schatten wird gebildet, welcher gibt zur architektonischen Arbeit ein gelassener oder dynamischer Charakter, aber immer stark expressiv.

Capturing light from above is a frequent design option, especially in trafficked places; with it you can explore different ways of relating to the environs and the landscape because, aside from allowing viewing of the sky, it increases the accumulation of heat in the interior and the resulting play of light and shadows indicates the course of the day and of the seasons of the year. The effect of light that barely touches the surface of the walls brings out their texture.

La captación de luz cenital es una opción de diseño frecuente, sobre todo en lugares de circulación; con ella se puede explorar una manera distinta de relacionarse con el entorno y el paisaje pues, aparte de permitir mirar el cielo, propicia la ganancia de calor para los interiores y el juego de claroscuros resultante va dejando constancia del curso del día y las estaciones del año. Los efectos de luz rasante sobre la superficie de los muros resalta las texturas de los mismos.

Le captage de la lumière zénithale est une option fréquente des designs du projet, surtout dans les lieux de circulation; avec elle, on peut explorer une manière différente de rapport avec l´entourage et le paysage car, en plus de permettre de regarder le ciel, elle favorise l'obtention de chaleur pour les intérieurs. De plus, le jeu de contrastes clair-obscur qui en résulte rend compte du cours du jour et des saisons de l´année. Les effets de la lumière rasante sur la surface des murs met en valeur leurs textures.

Der Empfang des Himmelslicht ist eine häufige Designmöglichkeit, dabei, in einem anderen Weg, Sie können die Umgebung und die Landschaft genießen, außer den Himmel anzuschauen, die Interieurs werden den Gewinn von Hitze haben und die resultierend Lichter und Schatten werden Beständigkeit vom Kurs vom Tag und den Stationen des Jahres verlassen. Die Wirkungen des Lichtes auf der Oberfläche der Mauern strecken ihre Texturen heraus.

The play of blind surfaces –walls– and large empty spaces –windows– in the resulting dimensions of the design of a house allows for experimenting with the lighting contributions that may occur between open and closed spaces; such is the case of relatively small patios that may be reasonably and comfortably illuminated with the light that comes from the interior spaces.

El juego de superficies ciegas –muros– y vacíos importantes –ventanas– en la volumetría resultante en el diseño de una casa, permite experimentar con las aportaciones luminosas que pueden sucederse entre los espacios abiertos y cerrados; tal es caso de patios relativamente pequeños que pueden quedar razonable y confortablemente iluminados con la luz proveniente de los interiores.

Le jeu des surfaces opaques –murs– et des vides importants –fenêtres– dans la volumétrie résultante du plan et design d'une maison, permet d'expérimenter avec les apports lumineux qui peuvent se succéder entre les espaces ouverts et fermés; comme c'est le cas des cours relativement petites qui peuvent rester raisonnablement et confortablement éclairées par la lumière provenant des espaces intérieurs.

Die Gruppe der blinden Oberflächen -Mauern- und wichtige Leere –Fenster- in den resultierend Dimensionen im Design eines Hauses, dies erlaubt mit den leuchtenden Beiträgen zwischen den offenen Räumen und geschlossen Räumen zu experimentieren; als die relativ kleinen Patios, welcher kann vernünftig und bequem mit dem Licht der Innere erleuchtet sein.

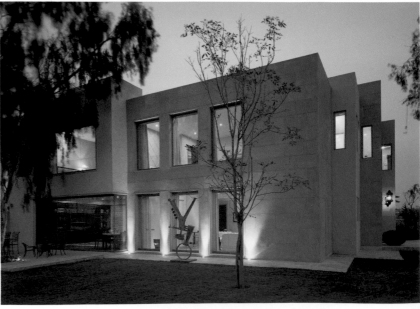

Generously illuminated spaces allow
for bringing out the details of the
architectural work, granting the whole a
feeling of spatial amplitude and liveliness.

Espacios generosamente iluminados
permiten resaltar los detalles de obra
dotando al conjunto de una sensación
de amplitud y vitalidad espacial.

Les espaces généreusement éclairés
permettent de mettre en valeur les détails
en donnant à l'ensemble une sensation
d'ampleur et de vitalité spatiale.

Räume erleuchteten großzügig,
die kann die Details der Arbeit
herausstrecken und dotiert es mit einer
Sensation von Weite und Raumenergie.

Nowadays, one of the fundamental considerations in interior design is to achieve sufficient, effective, warm and comfortable lighting, which at the same time does not involve major power consumption.

Hoy en día, una de las consideraciones fundamentales en los diseños de interiores es lograr una iluminación suficiente, eficiente, cálida y confortable, que al mismo tiempo no represente un consumo importante de energía.

De nos jours, une des préoccupations fondamentales dans les plans et designs d'intérieurs est d'obtenir un éclairage suffisant, efficace, chaleureux et confortable, qui, en même temps, ne représente pas une forte consommation d'énergie.

Heutzutage, eins der wesentlichen Überlegungen in das Interieurdesign ist die Leistung einer tüchtigen, warmer, bequemer und genug Illuminierung, und gleichzeitig stellt nicht wichtigen Verbrauch von Energie dar.

Proper treatment of natural or artificial light, combined with the particular shape of the space, help to give scale and personality to a given place.

El tratamiento adecuado de luz natural o artificial, sumado a las particulares condiciones de la forma del espacio, contribuye a darle escala y personalidad a un lugar determinado.

Le traitement adéquat de la lumière naturelle ou artificielle, allié aux conditions particulières de la forme de l'espace, contribue à donner échelle et personnalité à un lieu donné.

Die geeignete Behandlung natürlichen oder künstlichen Lichtes, und die bestimmten Zustände von der Form des Raumes geben Maßstab und Persönlichkeit zu einem bestimmten Raum.

The design of the different bodies and the facades of a house depends as much on their orientation as on aesthetic considerations. In some cases it is preferable to avoid windows and resort to games of dimension to create light and shadow effects; in some others, on the other hand, relationships between the interior and exterior spaces are established using large windows. The setup, dimensions and quantity of the windows determine the flow and quality of the natural light that enters and defines the introverted or outgoing personality of the building.

El diseño de los distintos cuerpos y de las fachadas de una casa dependen tanto de su orientación como de consideraciones estéticas. En algunos casos es preferible evitar las ventanas y recurrir a juegos de volúmenes para crear efectos de luz y sombra; en otros, en cambio, se establecen relaciones entre los espacios interiores y los exteriores mediante grandes ventanales. La disposición, dimensiones y cantidad de las ventanas determinan el flujo y la calidad de la luz natural que penetra al interior y definen el carácter introvertido o extrovertido de una construcción.

Le plan et design des divers éléments et des façades d'une maison dépendent autant de leur orientation que de considérations esthétiques. Dans certains cas, il est préférable d'éviter les fenêtres et de recourir à des jeux de volumes pour créer des effets de clair-obscur; dans d'autres, en revanche, les baies vitrées mettent en rapport les espaces intérieurs et extérieurs. La disposition, les dimensions et la quantité de fenêtres déterminent le flux et la qualité de la lumière naturelle qui pénètre à l'intérieur et définissent le caractère introverti ou extraverti d'un bâtiment.

Das Design von den verschiedenen Teilen und Fassaden eines Hauses hängt von ihrer Örtlichkeit sowie die ästhetischen Überlegungen ab. In einigen Fällen ist besser die Fenster zu vermeiden und schafft Wirkungen von Licht und Schatten mit verschiedenartigen Dimensionen; auf der anderen Seite, mit großen Fenstern kann das Haus Verbindungen zwischen Interieurs und Exterieurs haben. Die Disposition, Dimensionen und Qualität der Fenster bestimmen den Kurs und die Qualität des natürlichen Lichte, die penetrieret in das Interieur, und definiert den introvertiert oder extravertiert Charakter einer Konstruktion.

A house represents a unifying concept in design, but when the lighting of each of the spaces that make it up is treated with an emotional sense, this is clearly reflected in the general ambiance. So, through the lighting of an interior space, the calmness of exterior space can be achieved, or the effects of the exterior light can create emotions in the interior of the space. All of this is achieved if the lighting is designed thinking of the relationships between the inside and the outside, taking into consideration the course of light throughout the day.

Una casa representa un concepto unitario en el diseño, pero cuando la iluminación de cada uno de los espacios que la componen es tratado con un sentido emocional éste se refleja claramente en el ambiente general. Así, a través de la iluminación de un interior se puede conseguir la serenidad del espacio exterior, o bien los efectos de la luz del exterior pueden crear emociones al interior del espacio. Todo esto se consigue si se diseña la iluminación pensando en las relaciones entre el afuera y el adentro, y tomando en consideración los recorridos de luz en los distintos momentos del día.

Une maison représente un concept unitaire du plan et design, mais quand on envisage l'éclairage de chacun des espaces qui l'intègre dans son aspect émotionnel, cela se reflète clairement dans le cadre général. A travers l'éclairage d'un intérieur, on peut obtenir par là même une sérénité de l'espace extérieur, et les effets de la lumière extérieure peuvent créer des émotions au sein de l'espace. Tout cela est possible si l'on planifie l'éclairage en tenant compte des rapports entre l'extérieur et l'intérieur et du trajet de la lumière au cours de la journée.

Ein Haus repräsentiert ein einheitliches Konzept im Design, aber, wenn die Illuminierung von den Räumen des Hauses mit einem emotionalen Sinn behandelt wird, dies wird klar in der allgemeinen Atmosphäre widergespiegelt. Dieser Weg, durch die Illuminierung eines Interieur können Sie die Gelassenheit des äußeren Raumes bekommen, oder die Wirkungen vom Licht des Exterieur können Emotionen zum Innere des Raumes auch kreieren. All dies wird erreicht, wenn das Illuminationdesign erwägt das Interieur und das Exterieur, und die Wegkreuzungen des Lichtes in den verschiedenen Momenten des Tages.

living rooms
salas
salons
wohnzimmer

IN SOME INTERIOR DESIGNS, there are marked differences between the diverse types and functions of the spaces; in these cases, light can be useful for giving each space its own ambiance. It is also feasible to generate micro-atmospheres by modeling light in small corners of one space or bringing out luminous images on walls. To achieve this, it is possible to resort both to natural and artificial light.

EN ALGUNOS DISEÑOS DE INTERIORISMO se marcan diferencias entre los diversos tipos y funciones de los espacios de una casa; en estos casos, la luz puede ser de gran utilidad para que cada lugar cuente con su propio ambiente. También es factible generar micro atmósferas a través de la modelación de la luz en pequeños rincones de un mismo espacio o bien haciendo resaltar imágenes luminosas sobre muros. Para lograrlo, es posible valerse tanto de la iluminación natural como de la artificial.

DANS QUELQUES PLANS ET DESIGNS D'INTERIEURISME, on marque des différences entre les divers types et fonctions des espaces d'une maison; dans ce cas-là, la lumière peut être de grande utilité pour que chaque lieu dispose de son propre cadre. Il est également possible de créer des microatmosphères si l'on répartit la lumière en plusieurs petits coins d'un même espace ou bien si l'on projette des images lumineuses sur les murs. Pour ce faire, on peut aussi bien utiliser l'éclairage naturel quíartificiel.

IN EINIGES INTERIEUR DESIGNS, die Unterschiede zwischen den verschiedenartigen Arten und Funktionen von den Räumen eines Hauses werden markiert; in diesen Fällen, das Licht kann sehr nützlich sein, damit kann jeder Raum seine eigene Atmosphäre haben. Es ist auch durchführbar, die Generation von Mikro Atmosphäre durch die Behandlung des Lichtes in kleinen Ecken oder die Projektion leuchtender Bilder auf Mauern. Um dieses zu erreichen, es ist möglich, die natürliche und künstliche Illuminierung zu benutzen.

In the design of living spaces, it is necessary to consider the specific orientation of the place as well as the potential ways in which light may reach it; there are places with only artificial lighting or those which have a constant and direct presence of the sun.

En el diseño de los espacios de estar es necesario considerar las orientaciones específicas del lugar así como las distintas y posibles maneras de incidencia de la luz; hay lugares solamente iluminados o aquellos que cuentan además con la presencia constante y directa del sol.

Dans le plan et design des espaces de séjour, il faut prendre en compte les orientations spécifiques du lieu et les diverses manières possibles d'incidence de la lumière; il y a des lieux uniquement éclairés artificiellement et d'autres qui bénéficient en plus, de la présence constante et directe du soleil.

Im Design der Wohnzimmer ist notwendig ihre genaue L erwägen sowie die verschiedenartigen und mögliche W von Vorkommen des Lichtes; es gibt Zimmer, die nur erle sind oder es gibt auch Zimmer, die kontinuierliche und a Anwesenheit der Sonne haben.

The design of the lighting conditions of a house specifically depends on the lifestyle of each of its occupants. There will be those who prefer profusely lighted spaces or those who favor ambiances with low light. One can resort to different lighting methods; it is possible to choose direct or indirect lighting, as it is also possible to select the tones of the light –more or less warm- as preferred, including the type of light that can accentuate some details using colors in the light sources.

El diseño de las condiciones lumínicas de una casa depende específicamente de las maneras de vida de cada uno de los usuarios que la habitan. Habrá quienes prefieran los lugares profusamente iluminados o aquellos que gusten de ambientes con una cierta penumbra. Se puede recurrir a distintos modos de iluminación; es posible optar por una iluminación directa o indirecta, como también es factible seleccionar sobre las tonalidades de la luz –más o menos cálidas–, según se prefiera, incluyendo aquella con la que se pueden acentuar algunos detalles utilizando color en las luminarias.

Le plan des conditions d'éclairage d'une maison dépend tout particulièrement des modes de vie des usagers qui y habitent. Certains préféreront les lieux éclairés à profusion tandis que d'autres s'inclineront pour les cadres qui jouissent d'une certaine pénombre. On peut recourir à divers modes d'éclairage; on peut opter pour un éclairage direct ou indirect, et également sélectionner des tonalités lumineuses –plus ou moins chaleureuses–, selon ses goûts, et même une tonalité qui puisse accentuer certains détails grâce à l'usage de la couleur dans les luminaires.

Der Illuminationdesign eines Hauses hängt vom Lebensstil der Einwohner ab. Einige ziehen überreichlich erleuchtet Zimmer vor oder andere Leute ziehen Atmosphäre mit einer bestimmten Düsterheit vor. Es gibt verschiedene Arten von Illuminierung; es ist möglich, für eine direkte oder indirekte Illumination zu wählen, sowie es ist durchführbar, die Tonalitäten des Lichtes auszuwählen –mehr oder weniger warm–, als es vorgezogen wird, und sogar einige Details mit der Verwendung der Farbe in der Illumination zu akzentuieren.

In the transit spaces, using light captured by skylights is frequent, allowing that the main places of the house directly benefit from their light.

En los espacios de transición o circulaciones es frecuente la utilización de la luz captada a través de tragaluces, permitiendo así que los lugares importantes de la casa tomen de manera directa su iluminación.

Dans les espaces de transition ou de circulation, l'emploi de lucarnes et de vasistas pour capter la lumière est fréquent, car il permet que les lieux importants de la maison jouissent d'un éclairage direct.

Die Verwendung des Lichtes durch Dachfenster ist häufig In den Korridoren, dieser Weg, die wichtigen Räume des Hauses haben in einem direkten Weg ihre Illumination.

Sometimes stairways are essential elements in transit spaces. It is clear that one tries to have the best possible lighting in these spaces to make its function easier, especially when they do not have direct light from windows. At the same time, well-planned, natural and artificial lighting allows for creating the impression of generosity and space in these areas, and also brings out the expressive possibilities and the shapes associated with stairways, which are commonly very attractive.

En ocasiones las escaleras constituyen elementos esenciales en los espacios de circulación. Evidentemente se procura contar en estos lugares con la mejor iluminación posible para facilitar su funcionamiento, sobre todo cuando no cuentan con iluminación directa a través de ventanas. Al mismo tiempo, una estudiada iluminación, natural y artificial, permite crear sensaciones de generosidad y amplitud en estos espacios, resaltando también las posibilidades expresivas y formales asociadas con las escaleras, que por lo general resultan muy atractivas.

Parfois, les escaliers constituent les éléments essentiels des espaces de circulation. Il faut bien sûr veiller à ce que ces lieux bénéficient du meilleur éclairage possible pour faciliter leur fonctionnement, surtout quand ils ne disposent pas d'une illumination directe des fenêtres. Dans le même temps, un éclairage étudié, naturel et artificiel, permet de créer dans ces espaces des sensations de générosité et d'ampleur, et met en également en valeur les possibilités expressives et formelles associées aux escaliers, qui, en général, sont très attrayantes.

Die Treppen sind erforderliche Elemente in einem Haus. Augenscheinlich brauchen diese die beste mögliche Illumination, ihre Bedienung zu erleichtern, hauptsächlich, wenn sie keine direkte Illumination durch Fenster haben. Im selben Augenblick, eine gute natürliche und künstliche Illumination kreiert Sensationen von Großzügigkeit und Weite in diesen Räumen, außer streckt die ausdrucksvollen und formellen Möglichkeiten heraus, die mit den Treppen verbunden werden, welche sind gewöhnlich sehr attraktiv.

Transit spaces should not necessarily be considered at their minimum functional and dimensional expression. When it is feasible to give them more space they can become potential galleries, which, bare or featuring paintings and sculptures, emphasize and give more importance to their presence. Light contributes to bringing out the dimensional compositions and the spatial continuity natural to these spaces, and it also allows emphasizing the textures, color palettes, quality, and diversity of materials and the solution of specific details that accompany them.

No necesariamente los lugares de transición pueden o deben ser considerados en su mínima expresión funcional y dimensional. Cuando es factible que cuenten con mayor amplitud se pueden convertir en posibles galerías, que desnudas o alojando cuadros y esculturas logran enfatizar y dar importancia a su presencia. La luz colabora en destacar las composiciones volumétricas y las continuidades espaciales que son naturales a estos lugares, y también permite enfatizar las texturas, gamas de colores, calidad, diversidad de materiales y solución de detalles específicos que los acompañan.

Les lieux de transition ne doivent pas forcément être envisagés dans leur stricte expression fonctionnelle et dimensionnelle. Quand il est possible qu'ils soient plus spacieux, ils peuvent devenir des galeries qui, nues ou décorées de tableaux et de sculptures, parviennent à mettre en valeur et donner de l'importance à leur présence. La lumière collabore à mettre l'accent sur les compositions volumétriques et les continuités spatiales qui sont naturelles à ces lieux. Elle permet également de mettre en valeur les textures, les gammes de couleurs, la qualité, la diversité des matériaux et la résolution de détails spécifiques qui les accompagnent.

Die Korridore sollten in ihrem minimalen zweckmäßigen und dimensionalen Ausdruck nicht erwägtet werden, es ist nicht notwendig. Wenn große Weite haben, sie können mögliche Galerien werden, mit oder ohne Bilder und Skulpturen kann betonen und geben Wichtigkeit zu ihrer Anwesenheit. Das Licht hebt das dimensionalen Werk und die Raumkontinuitäten hervor, welche sind natürlich zu diesen Räumen, und betont die Texturen, Farben, Qualität, Vielfalt von Materialien und Lösung spezifischer Details.

The presence or lack of furniture, as well as its quantity, array, and the quality of its finish, help light as a whole to give presence and personality to a given space.

La presencia o ausencia de mobiliario, su cantidad, disposición, incluyendo la calidad de sus terminados, contribuyen conjuntamente con la luz a darle presencia y carácter a un espacio determinado.

La présence ou absence de mobilier, sa quantité, sa disposition, et même la qualité de sa finition, contribuent avec la lumière à donner une présence et du caractère à un espace donné.

Die Anwesenheit oder Abwesenheit des Möbel, ihre Quantität, Disposition, und inklusive die Qualität, gemeinsam tragen sie mit dem Licht bei, um einem bestimmten Raum zu verschönern und zu charakterisieren.

The ornamental elements contribute to giving life to spaces. Likewise, it is possible to find details with the proper light for highlighting them.

Los elementos decorativos colaboran en dar vida a los espacios. De igual manera es posible llegar al detalle considerando la luz adecuada para resaltarlos.

Les éléments décoratifs contribuent à donner vie aux espaces. De même, il est possible de soigner les détails si l'on dispose de la lumière adéquate pour les mettre en valeur.

Die dekorativen Elemente heben die Räume hervor. So gut wie, das geeignete Licht ist ein großes Detail, um sie herauszustrecken.

It is important to consider the sequence of the different areas in the architectural design of a house, because they become, for those who live in them, part of the daily revelations of the space. The different qualities of light can accompany and classify different places on its path, marking or suggesting a sense of continuity, direction or permanence. The dimensions of each place, as well as its functional characteristics and the potential views towards the outside, determine the needs and characteristics of the light required.

Es importante considerar las secuencias de las distintas áreas en el diseño arquitectónico de una casa, pues éstas se convierten, para quien las vive, en parte de las revelaciones cotidianas del espacio. Las diferentes calidades de luz pueden ir acompañando y calificando los diversos lugares durante los recorridos, marcando o induciendo un sentido de continuidad, dirección o permanencia. Las dimensiones de cada lugar, además de sus características funcionales y las posibilidades de vistas hacia el exterior, determinan los requerimientos y características de la luz necesaria.

Dans le plan architectonique, il est important de considérer l'ensemble en prenant en compte les séquences spatiales grâce auxquelles on découvre et vit une œuvre déterminée. Les différences concernant la qualité de la lumière peuvent qualifier les divers types de lieux dans leurs trajets possibles, en marquant ou induisant un sens de continuité, de directionnalité ou de permanence. Les dimensions de chaque lieu, en plus de leurs caractéristiques fonctionnelles et les possibilités de vues vers l'extérieur, déterminent les exigences et caractéristiques de la lumière nécessaire.

Im architektonischen Design ist wichtig alles zu erwägen, sowie die Sequenz des Raumes, um bestimmte Arbeit zu entdecken und zu leben. Die Unterschiede der Qualitäten des Lichtes können die verschiedenen Orte in den möglichen Wegen qualifizieren, die markieren oder veranlassen einen Sinn von Kontinuität, Richtung oder Dauerhaftigkeit. Die Dimensionen jedes Raumes, außerdem ihren zweckmäßigen Merkmalen und den Möglichkeiten von Sichten zum Exterieur, bestimmen die Anforderungen und Merkmale des notwendigen Lichtes.

JUST AS IN THE CASE OF THE LIVING ROOMS OF A HOUSE, dining rooms in general are designed seeking the best views to the outside, which helps them to have generous natural lighting that fills the space with life. When it comes to using artificial lighting, it is possible to witness the creation of different atmospheres, taking advantage of the possibilities offered by modern lighting systems and equipment, which, when applied properly, mold virtually any space in terms of brightness.

AL IGUAL QUE PARA LAS SALAS DE UNA CASA, por lo general los comedores se diseñan buscando las mejores vistas hacia el exterior, con lo que se logra que los interiores cuenten con una generosa iluminación natural que impregne de vitalidad al espacio. En lo que concierne al empleo de la luz artificial es posible contemplar la creación de diferentes atmósferas aprovechando las

posibilidades que ofrecen las características de los sistemas y equipos de iluminación actuales, que aplicados de forma adecuada permiten modelar prácticamente cualquier espacio en términos de luminosidad.

COMME POUR LES SALLES DE SEJOUR D'UNE MAISON, en général, on planifie les salles à manger en cherchant les meilleures vues vers l'extérieur, pour que, de cette façon, les intérieurs bénéficient d'un généreux éclairage naturel qui imprègne vitalité à l'espace. En ce qui concerne l'emploi de la lumière artificielle, on peut envisager la création d'atmosphères différentes si l'on profite des possibilités qu'offrent les caractéristiques des systèmes et des équipements d'éclairage actuels, qui, appliqués convenablement, permettent de modeler pratiquement nîimporte quel lieu en termes de luminosité.

NORMALERWEISE, DIE ESSZIMMER UND DIE WOHNZIMMER in ihrem Design suchen die besten Sichten zum Äußere, Dieser Weg, die Interieurs haben eine natürliche Illumination, die mit Energie der Raum schwängert. Über die Verwendung des künstlichen Lichtes, es ist möglich, die Schaffung verschiedenartiger Atmosphäre zu betrachten, die Möglichkeiten von den Merkmalen von den Systemen und Ausstattungen des Illumination auszunutzen, so gut wie irgendeinen Raum in Hinsicht auf Glanz zu modellieren, alles in einem geeigneten Weg.

dining rooms
comedores
salles à manger
eßzimmer

To design the lighting of a space, one can consider the light coming in from outside, which enters through windows, domes and skylights, as well as light from the lamps on the furniture, which are fixed and placed in walls or plafonds. It is possible to add to this, also as part of the lighting design, the effects caused by the reflections coming from walls finished in light colors, as well as those from shiny surfaces, floors or walls.

Para diseñar la iluminación de un espacio se puede tomar en cuenta la luz proveniente del exterior que penetra a través de las ventanas, domos y tragaluces, así como las luces de las lámparas que conforman el mobiliario y aquellas que se encuentran fijas y que se ubican en muros o plafones. Es factible sumar a lo anterior, también como parte del diseño de iluminación, los efectos causados por los reflejos provenientes de los muros terminados en colores claros como también aquellas otras que resultan de las superficies brillantes, de pisos o muros.

Pour planifier l'éclairage d'un lieu, on peut profiter de la lumière provenant de l'extérieur qui pénètre par les fenêtres, les dômes, les lucarnes et vasistas. On peut également tenir compte des éclairages des lampes qui font partie du mobilier et des lampes fixes qui se trouvent sur les murs ou les plafonds. Il convient d'ajouter à cela, car ils font également partie du plan d'éclairage, les effets provoqués par les reflets des murs de couleurs claires et par ceux qui résultent des surfaces brillantes, des sols ou des murs.

Um die Illumination eines Raumes zu entwerfen wir können das Licht des Exterieur erwägen, die kommt durch Fenster, Kuppeln und Dachfenster herein, sowie die Lichter von den Lampen des Möbel, und jene, die stabil sind, und in Mauern oder Deckenlampen-Rosetten. All dies ist Teil des Illuminationdesign, die Effekten von den Spiegelungen der Mauern mit weichen Farben, sowie die Effekten der glänzenden Oberflächen von Böden oder Mauern.

kitchens   cocinas   cuisines   küchen

For the design of the spaces meant for the preparation of food, a proper balance between natural and artificial lighting is important, light which should fall directly on the workspaces.

Para el diseño de los espacios destinados a la preparación de alimentos es importante un balance adecuado entre la iluminación natural y artificial, incidiendo de manera directa en las áreas de trabajo.

Pour le plan et design des espaces destinés à la préparation des aliments, il est important de trouver un équilibre adéquat entre l'éclairage naturel et artificiel, lequel répercute de manière directe sur les lieux de travail.

Für das Küchendesign, es ist wichtig ein geeignetes Gleichgewicht zwischen der natürlichen und künstlichen Illumination, um in einem direkten Weg in den Arbeitszimmern zu beeinflussen.

THE MODERN KITCHEN SHOWS the significant impact of specialization on the subject; the incorporation of a style of lighting that allows the faithful contemplation of the nature of the ingredients with which food is prepared is considered to be an integral part of the conditions of design of the different furniture that make it up.

EN LOS PROYECTOS MODERNOS DE COCINAS ha tenido un impacto importante el alto grado de especialización en la materia; como parte integral de las condiciones de diseño de los distintos muebles que las componen, tomando además en cuenta la incorporación de una iluminación que permita la apreciación fiel de la naturaleza de los ingredientes con los que se prepara la comida.

DANS LES PROJETS MODERNES DE CUISINES, le haut degré de spécialisation dans la matière a eu une répercussion importante. Partie intégrante des conditions du design des différents meubles qui les conforment, l'éclairage doit permettre l'appréciation fidèle de la nature des ingrédients qul composent les plats.

IN DEN MODERNEN PROJEKTEN DER KÜCHEN; der hohe Spezialisierunggrad in der Sache hat eine wichtige Wirkung gehabt; als wesentlicher Teil der Design Zuständen vom verschiedenartigen Möbel, das sie zusammensetzen, wir erwägen die Einverleibung einer Illumination, welcher erlaubt die treue Würdigung der Natur von den Bestandteilen, die man für das Essen vorbereitet.

baths
baños
salles de bains
badmer

WITH THE PURPOSE OF CREATING A FEELING of space in the bathrooms, artificial light can be used in combination with the direct entrance of natural light, captured through windows or domes, and reflected with mirrors. The spatial game that arises from this combination of light and reflecting surfaces creates an aesthetic impression that influences the perception of the space. When these factors are complemented with contemporary bathroom furniture with sober lines, spaces of great functionality and comfort are achieved.

CON LA FINALIDAD DE CREAR UNA IMPRESIÓN de amplitud en los espacios de los baños se puede utilizar la luz artificial en combinación con la incidencia directa de luz natural, captada a través de ventanas o domos y reflejada mediante grandes espejos. El juego espacial que surge de esta combinación de luz y superficies reflejantes crea una sensación estética que influye en la percepción del espacio. Cuando estos factores se complementan con muebles sanitarios contemporáneos, de líneas sobrias, se concretan espacios de gran funcionalidad y comodidad.

DANS LE BUT DE CREER UNE IMPRESSION d'ampleur dans les espaces des salles de bains, on peut utiliser la lumière artificielle et également l'incidence directe de la lumière naturelle, captée par les fenêtres ou les dômes, qui se reflète grâce à de grands miroirs. Le jeu spatial produit de cette combinaison de lumière et de surfaces réfléchissantes crée une sensation esthétique qui influe sur la perception de l'espace. Quand ces facteurs se complètent par des meubles de bain contemporains, aux lignes sobres, des espaces de grande fonctionnalité et commodité prennent corps.

UM EINEN EINDRUCK VON WEITE in den Räumen der Badezimmer zu kreieren, wir können das künstliche Licht in Kombination mit dem direkten Vorkommen natürlichen Lichtes benutzen, fing durch Fenster oder Kuppeln und spiegelte mittels großer Spiegel. Die Raumspiel, die von dieser Kombination von Licht und leuchtenden Oberflächen erscheint, kreiert eine ästhetische Sensation, die in der Wahrnehmung des Raumes beeinflußt. Wenn diese Faktoren mit zeitgenössischem sanitärem Möbel ergänzt werden, es wird Räume von großer Funktionalität und Bequemlichkeit erhalten.

The trend is frequently to create very illuminated spaces, combined with the use of light colors, polished surfaces and the division of large materials and furniture, the details resolved with simple and regular geometric shapes, for the purpose of creating atmospheres of great neatness and order, obviously desirable for these places of hygiene. It is worth mentioning, that these solutions avoid the presence of seams and nooks that would be difficult to maintain and clean.

Es frecuente la tendencia a crear espacios muy iluminados, combinados con el uso de colores claros, superficies pulidas y despiece de materiales de gran tamaño, así como mobiliario y detalles resueltos con formas geométricas simples y regulares, con la finalidad de generar atmósferas de pulcritud y orden, evidentemente deseables para estos lugares de aseo. Vale la pena destacar, en este mismo sentido, que mediante las soluciones antes mencionadas se procura evitar la existencia de juntas y recovecos que se conviertan en lugares de difícil mantenimiento y limpieza.

La tendance est à la création d'espaces très éclairés, combinés à des couleurs claires, des surfaces polies et des matériaux de grande taille, et à un mobilier et des éléments aux formes géométriques simples et régulières, dans le but de générer des atmosphères soignées et ordonnées, qui sont évidemment souhaitables pour ces lieux de toilette. Cela vaut la peine de souligner, dans ce sens, que, grâce aux solutions mentionnées, on essaie d'éviter l'existence de joints et de recoins qui deviennent des lieux d'entretien et de nettoyage difficiles.

Ist häufig, sehr erleuchtet Räume zu kreieren, kombinierte mit der Verwendung kombinierte mit der Verwendung weicher Farben, verfeinert Oberflächen und das Vierteln von großen Materialien, sowie Möbel und Details mit geometrischen, einfachen und regulären Formen, um Atmosphäre von Ordentlichkeit und Reinlichkeit zu erzeugen, augenscheinlich wünschenswert für diese Zimmer. Mittels der Lösungen vor erwähnte, wir versuchen die Existenz von Schlupfwinkeln und Ecken zu vermeiden, das heißt, Räume schwieriger Aufrechterhaltung und Sauberkeit zu vermeiden.

Industrial design has had a great impact when it comes to bathroom furniture and accessories, some of them becoming authentic sculptures, without neglecting their functional requirements. Such is the case with washbasins and the different lines of faucets that flood the market these days, produced in materials of high visual quality, such as stainless steel, glass or onyx.

El diseño industrial ha tenido un gran impacto en lo referente a mobiliario y accesorios de baño, llegando a convertirse muchos de ellos en verdaderas piezas escultóricas, sin descuidar sus requerimientos funcionales. Tal es el caso de los lavabos y las distintas líneas de grifería que hoy abundan en el mercado, producidas en materiales de alta calidad visual, como el acero inoxidable, el cristal o el onix.

Le design industriel a eu une grande répercussion sur le mobilier et les accessoires de bain, dont un grand nombre devient de véritables pièces sculpturales, sans pour autant négliger leurs exigences fonctionnelles. Tel est le cas des lavabos et des diverses lignes de robinetterie, aux matériaux de haute qualité visuelle, comme l'acier inoxydable, le cristal ou l'onyx, qui foisonnent aujourd'hui sur le marché.

Das industrielle Design hat eine große Wirkung hinsichtlich Badezimmermöbel und Zubehöre gehabt, welche sind wahre bildhauerische Stücke geworden, ohne ihrer zweckmäßigen Anforderungen zu vernachlässigen. Als die Waschbecken und die verschiedenartigen Wasserhähne, die existieren heute in großer Quantität im Markt, produzierte in Materialien großer visueller Qualität, zum Beispiel der Edelstahl, das Glas oder der Onyx.

PERGOLAS ARE FREQUENTLY USED ON TERRACES for avoiding the direct impact of sunrays. The design of this kind of protection offers great possibilities for formal experimentation, because there is a large gamut of materials with which they can be built, whether metal or wood, and different degrees of light reduction that can be achieved. The best examples are those that harmonize with the design criteria of the architectural work as a whole and in which the building details are cared for.

ES FRECUENTE EL USO DE PÉRGOLAS EN LAS TERRAZAS con el objeto de evitar la incidencia directa de los rayos solares. El diseño de este tipo de protecciones ofrece extensas posibilidades de experimentación formal, pues es muy amplio el espectro de materiales, ya sean metales o maderas,

con los que pueden construirse, así como los diferentes grados de reducción de la luz que pueden lograrse. Los mejores ejemplos son aquellos cuyas soluciones armonizan con los criterios de diseño del conjunto de la obra y en los que se presta cuidado a los detalles constructivos.

L'EMPLOI DE PERGOLAS DANS LES TERRASSES, afin d'éviter l'incidence directe des rayons solaires, est fréquent. Le plan et design de ce type de protections offre d'énormes possibilités díexpérimentation formelle, car le spectre de matériaux avec lesquels on peut les construire, que ce soit des métaux ou des bois, de même que les divers degrés de réduction de la lumière qu'on peut obtenir, est très vaste. Les meilleurs exemples sont ceux dont les solutions sont en harmonie avec les critères du plan et design de l'ensemble de l'œvre et où on fait attention aux détails de construction.

ES IST HÄUFIG, PERGOLAS IN DEN TERRASSEN zu benutzen, um das direkte Vorkommen der solaren Strahlen zu vermeiden. Das Design dieser Schutze bieten viele Möglichkeiten formellen Experimentieren an, weil das Spektrum von Materialien sehr breit ist, baute mit Metallen oder Holz, sowie die anderen Verkleinerunggrad vom Licht, das erreicht werden kann. Die besten Beispiele sind jene, wessen Lösungen mit den Designkriterien der ganzen Arbeit harmonisieren und jene hinsichtlich zu den konstruktiven Details.

terraces
terrazas
terrasses
terrassen

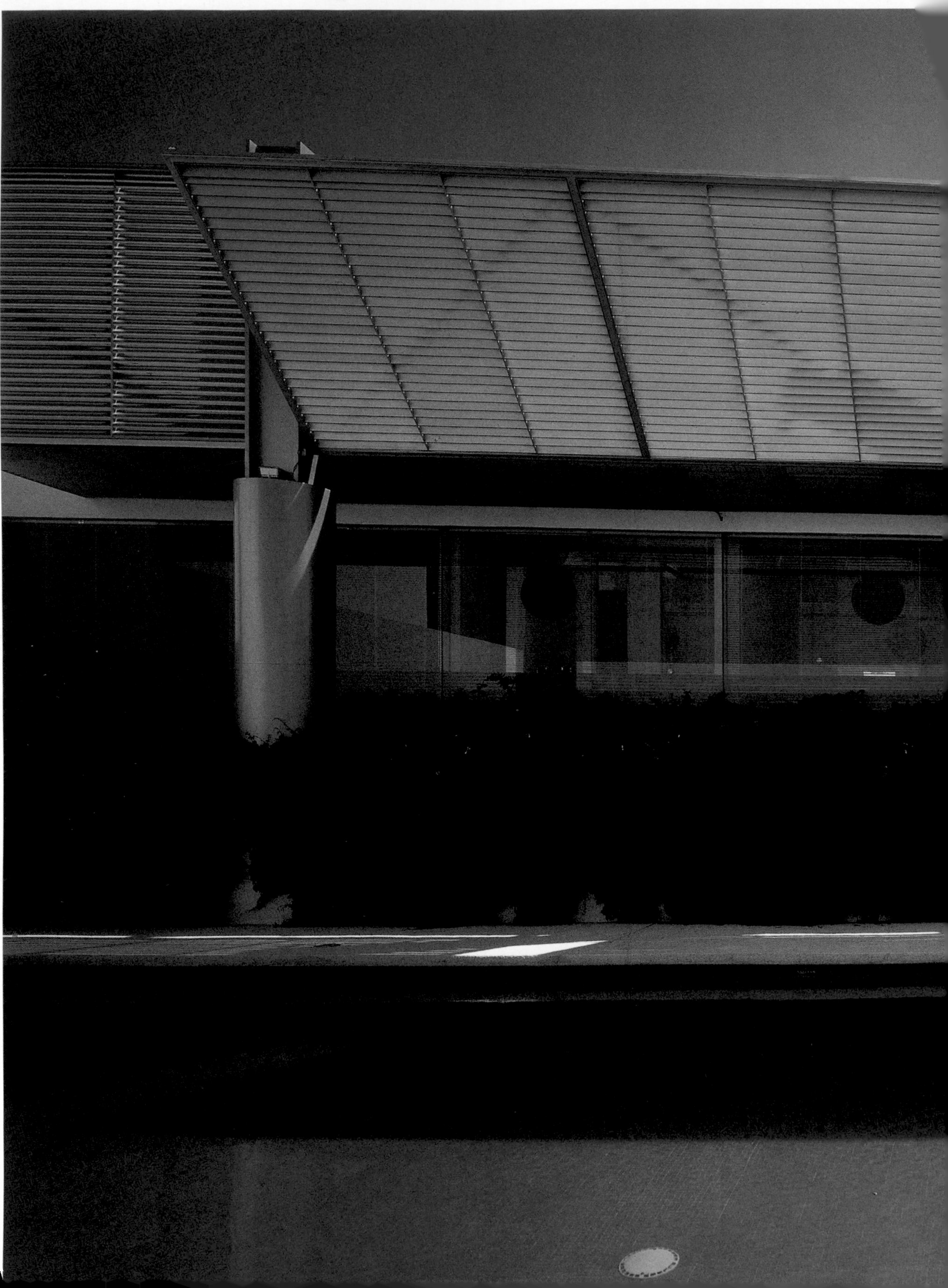

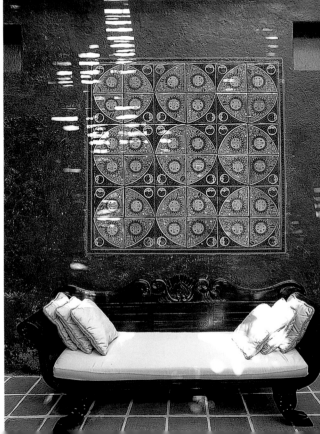

The yard or terrace space may be qualified by the direct impact of the sun or by light filtered through woven covers, creating dynamic games of light and shadow that let the colors and textures of the dominant surfaces stand out.

El espacio de patios o terrazas puede estar calificado por la incidencia directa del sol o por la luz tamizada que se filtra a través de cubiertas caladas, provocando juegos dinámicos de claroscuros que dejan resaltar los colores y texturas de las superficies dominantes.

L'espace des cours ou des terrasses peut être influencé par l'incidence directe du soleil ou par la lumière tamisée qui filtre à travers des couvertures percées, ce qui entraîne des jeux dynamiques de clairs-obscurs qui mettent en valeur les couleurs et les textures des surfaces dominantes.

Die Patios oder Terrassen können das direkte Vorkommen der Sonne haben, oder auch gesiebte Licht zu haben, dieser Weg, wir erhalten dynamische Gruppen von Lichtern und Schatten, die herausstrecken die Farben und Texturen der dominierenden Oberflächen.

Within the possible alternatives for the design of terraces, light allows for accentuating the different qualities and transitions of spaces, differentiating the inside from the outside. Other design possibilities show spaces of an ambivalent nature, in the sense that they give the occupant the impression of being inside even when he is outside; this is achieved through the use of linear wefts that create the illusion of being continuously covered, without it being necessarily true.

Dentro de las alternativas posibles de diseño de terrazas, la luz permite acentuar las distintas calidades y transiciones del espacio, diferenciando el adentro del afuera. Otras posibilidades de diseño muestran espacios con carácter ambivalente, en el sentido de que logran que el usuario tenga la sensación de estar adentro aún cuando en realidad se encuentre afuera; esto se logra con tramas lineales que crean la ilusión visual de estar bajo cubiertas continuas, sin que ello sea necesariamente cierto.

Parmi les alternatives possibles de plan et design de terrasses, la lumière permet de mettre en valeur les diverses qualités et transitions de l'espace, en différenciant l'intérieur de l'extérieur. D'autres possibilités de plan montrent des espaces au caractère ambivalent, dans le sens où ils donnent à l'usager la sensation d'être à l'intérieur même si, en réalité, il se trouve dehors. On obtient cet effet en utilisant des trames linéaires qui créent l'illusion optique d'être sous des couvertures continues, sans que ce soit pour autant vrai.

In den möglichen Alternativen von das Design der Terrassen, das Licht akzentuiertet die verschiedenartigen Qualitäten und Übergänge des Raumes, unterscheidet den Innere und den Äußere auch. Andere Design Möglichkeiten zeigen Räume mit ambivalentem Charakter, wo der Benutzer sich fühlt, daß innen ist, sogar wenn in der Wirklichkeit ist draußen; wegen die geradlinige Weben, welcher kreiert die visuelle Illusion fortlaufender Decken, obwohl es nicht notwendigerweise wahr ist.

design
diseño

THERE IS AN INCREASING awareness among people of the importance of establishing and executing a good design for achieving the house they wish to live in. It is evident that, to achieve it, it is essential to consider the material, spiritual and psychological needs of the occupants of the house. The peculiarities of the environs where the future dwelling is to be located also should be considered, such as the views and the quality of the neighboring buildings, as well as weather conditions: sun exposure, rain, average temperature and dominant winds in the area.

exteriors
exteriores
extérieurs
außen

ENTRE LA GENTE existe cada vez más conciencia de la importancia de fundamentar e instrumentar un buen diseño para lograr la casa en la que se desea vivir. Evidentemente, para alcanzar lo anterior, es esencial considerar las necesidades materiales, espirituales y psicológicas del o los usuarios que habitarán la casa. Se deben tomar también en cuenta las particularidades del entorno donde se ubicará la futura vivienda, tales como vistas y calidad de las construcciones vecinas, así como las condiciones del clima: asoleamientos, lluvia, temperatura promedio y vientos dominantes de la zona.

DE NOS JOURS, les gens ont de plus en plus conscience de l'importance de jeter les fondements et d'effectuer un bon plan et design afin de pouvoir réaliser la maison qu'ils désirent habiter. Pour atteindre cet objectif, il faut évidemment tenir compte des besoins matériels, spirituels et psychologiques des futurs usagers de la maison. Il faut également prendre en compte les spécificités de l'environnement du futur logement, notamment l'apparence et la qualité des constructions avoisinantes, et les conditions climatiques: ensoleillement, précipitations, température moyenne et vents dominants de la région.

LEUTE SIND immer mehr bewusst über den Design des Haus wo Sie leben möchten. Um das obengenannte zu erreichen, muss man selbstverständlich die materiellen, geistigen und psychologischen Notwendigkeiten des Benutzer, die das Haus bewohnen werden. Umgebung, wo das künftige Haus angesiedellt wird, wie zum Beispiel die Aussicht und die Qualität der benachbarten Konstruktionen sowie die Zustände des Klimas: sonnige, regnerische, durchsnittliche Temperatur und dominerende Wind des Gebietes.

In the design of a house, the combination and interrelation of interior and exterior spaces is feasible and desirable, and it may be enhanced by patios with water surfaces. Water provides freshness to the spaces, and at the same time it reflects the architectural work, as well as the light that falls upon it during the day or emerges from it during the night. In some buildings, with dimensions of strong and clear geometry, this reflection gains a fundamental importance in the conception of the project and grants it a distinguishing mark.

En el diseño de una casa es factible y deseable la combinación e interrelación de espacios exteriores e interiores, cuyo interés se puede incrementar mediante patios con espejos de agua. El agua proporciona frescura a los ambientes, a la vez que reproduce la obra arquitectónica, así como la luz que la baña de día o que surge de ella en la noche. En algunas construcciones, con volúmenes de fuerte y nítida geometría, este reflejo adquiere una importancia fundamental en la concepción del proyecto otorgándole un sello distintivo.

Dans le design d'une maison, la combinaison et l'interrelation des espaces extérieurs et intérieurs est possible et même souhaitable. Cette combinaison peut redoubler d'intérêt si l'on intégre des patios avec des plans d'eau. L'eau donne, en effet, de la fraîcheur à l'environnement et reflète aussi l'œuvre architectonique et la lumière qui la baigne durant la journée ou qui émane la nuit. Dans certaines constructions aux volumes géométriques forts et nets, ce reflet acquiert une importance fondamentale dans la conception du projet car il lui confère une marque distinctive.

Die Kombination und gegenseitige Beziehung von Exterieur und Interieur Räume sind durchführbar und wünschenswert im Design eines Hauses, wessen Interesse mittels Patios mit Wasserspiegeln zunehmen kann. Wasser gibt Frische zur Atmosphäre, und reproduziert gleichzeitig die architektonische Arbeit, sowie das Tag-und Nachtlicht. In einigen Konstruktionen mit großer Dimensionen und klarer Geometrie erwirbt diese Spiegelung eine wesentliche Wichtigkeit in der Vorstellung des Projektes der einen auffälligen Stil gewährt.

It is feasible to treat the exteriors as green spaces or as calm, austere yards that can be finished by taking advantage of the progress of modern technology applied to timber, which allows it to be exposed to weather and to even have controlled contact with water bodies in conditions of reliability and durability, achieving an ambience of great living quality.

Es factible tratar los exteriores como espacios verdes o como patios serenos, austeros, que pueden ser terminados aprovechando los adelantos de la tecnología moderna aplicados a la industria de la madera, que permite en condiciones de confiabilidad y duración su exposición a la intemperie e incluso su contacto controlado con cuerpos de agua, logrando ambientes de gran calidad vivencial.

Les extérieurs peuvent être employés comme espaces verts ou comme cours sereines et austères. Ils peuvent être réalisés grâce aux progrès de la technologie moderne appliqués à l'industrie du bois, laquelle permet, dans des conditions de sécurité et de longévité, leur exposition aux intempéries et même le contact contrôlé avec des corps liquides, obtenant ainsi un environnement de grande qualité de vie.

Es ist durchführbar, der Exterieur als grüne Räume zu behandeln oder als gelassene und strenge Patios, welcher mit den Fortschritten moderner Technologie beendet werden kann. Diese Technologie ist zur Industrie des Holzes angewandt. Das erlaubt seine Entblößung zum Wetter und sogar der kontrollierte Kontakt mit dem Wasser, die den Umgebung eine größer Qualität erreicht.

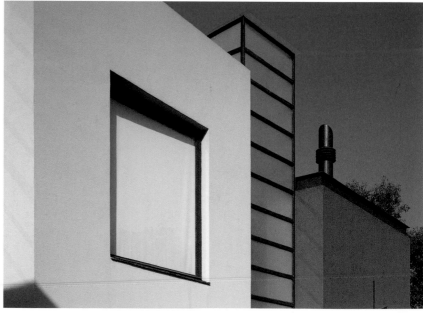

Changes in level, materials, texture, color and light quality can generate distinctive ambiances in exterior design.

Los cambios de nivel, materiales, textura, color y calidad luminosa pueden generar ambientes diferenciados en el diseño de exteriores.

Les changements de niveau, de matériaux, de texture, de couleur et de qualité lumineuse peuvent générer des cadres différenciés dans le design des extérieurs.

Die Veränderungen des Niveaus, Materialien, Textur, Farbe und leuchtende Qualität können unterschiedene Umgebungen im Exterieur Design erzeugen.

It always is an interesting challenge to achieve a good design that makes reference to tradition when it comes to materials and lifestyles, but without forgetting the commitment to modernity.

Siempre es un reto interesante lograr un buen diseño que tenga referencias con la tradición en cuanto a materiales y modos de vida, pero sin renunciar al compromiso que existe con la modernidad.

Réaliser de projects et designs qui soient en accord avec la tradition, quant aux matériaux et modes de vie, mais sans pour autant renoncer à l'engagement vis-à-vis de la modernité, est sans nul doute un défi intéressant.

Es ist immer eine interessante Herausforderung, ein gutes Design auf zu erreichen. Der Design soll die Tradition bezüglich Materialien und Lebensstile übergeben, ohne der existente Verpflichtung mit der Modernität löschen.

It is feasible to protect facades from direct rainfall with small overhangs, preventing damage to the paint during the rainy season.

Es factible que a través de pequeños volados se proteja a las fachadas de la caída directa de la lluvia, evitando daños a la pintura.

On peut protéger les façades de la chute directe de la pluie grâce à de petits auvents, afin que la peinture ne s'endommage pas pendant la saison des pluies.

Die kleinen Dächer sind ratsam und schützen die Fassaden vom direkten Sturz. Damit vermeiden Schadensersatz zum Gemälde während der regnerischen Jahreszeit.

Doors are, by their own right, connecting and transition elements between the exterior and interior of a house, and thus become focal points of the design. Blind doors, which prevent viewing the inside from outside, are preferably used when an implied separation between these two spaces is wanted or else when demanded for purposes of safety and privacy. Doors with transparencies, on the other hand, allow for visual continuity, linking both spaces.

Las puertas son, por excelencia, elementos de conexión y transición entre el exterior y el interior de una casa, y por lo tanto se convierten en puntos focales del diseño. Las puertas ciegas, en las que se evita las visuales entre interior y exterior, se usan preferentemente cuando se desea lograr una separación franca entre estos ambientes o bien cuando las condiciones de seguridad y privacidad así lo demandan. Las puertas con transparencias, en cambio, permiten la continuidad visual ligando ambos espacios.

Les portes sont, par excellence, des éléments de connexion et de transition entre l'extérieur et l'intérieur d'une maison, et elles sont, par conséquent, des points focaux du plan et design. Les portes opaques, qui obstruent la vue entre l'intérieur et l'extérieur, s'utilisent de préférence quand on désire faire une séparation tacite de ces espaces, ou bien lorsque les conditions de sécurité et d'intimité le requièrent. En revanche, les portes transparentes lient ces deux espaces et permettent ainsi la continuité visuelle.

Die Türen sind Brennpunkte im Design, weil sie den Verbindung- und Übergang- Elemente zwischen dem Außen und dem Interieur eines Hauses sind. Die blinden Türen, die die Vergegenwärtigung zwischen Interieur und Exterieur vermieden sind, sind vorzugsweise für eine stille Trennung zwischen die Atmosphären oder wenn die Sicherheitzustände und Privatsphärezustände es erfordern. Auf der anderen Seite erlauben die Türen mit Transparenzen die visuelle Kontinuität und verbinden beide Räume.

living rooms salas salons wohnzimmer

For spaces meant for family and social life, treatments based on double heights are suitable, with generous lighting, with possible continuity towards other public spaces.

Para los espacios destinados a la convivencia familiar y los amigos, resultan propicios los tratamientos con base en dobles alturas, generosamente iluminados, con posibles continuidades -hacia otros lugares de carácter público.

Pour les espaces destinés à vie familiale et amicale, les traitements avec une base de double hauteur, généreusement éclairés, et avec des prolongements possibles vers d'autres lieux publics, sont adéquats.

Die doppelten Höhen sind günstig für die Räume der Familienereignisse und Freunden, großzügig erleuchtete, mit Kontinuität zu anderen öffentlichen Plätze.

WHEN THE LIVING AND DINING SPACES have large glass surfaces that allow for seeing the outside, a relationship of interior-exterior continuity can be established, and it is also possible to enjoy the design of the landscape and favor the entrance of natural light; these elements sometimes become dynamic, living frames that give the occupants a feeling of more space. When it comes to work or study spaces, partial or total isolation with screens or partition walls can help concentration on the activity.

CUANDO LOS LUGARES DE ESTAR Y COMER cuentan con grandes superficies acristaladas que permiten las visuales hacia el exterior se puede establecer una relación de continuidad interior-exterior, disfrutar del diseño de paisaje y favorecer la entrada de luz natural; estos elementos en ocasiones se convierten en dinámicos cuadros vitales que brindan a los usuarios una sensación de mayor amplitud. En el caso de los lugares de trabajo o estudio, el aislamiento parcial o total a través del uso de mamparas o muros que subdividen el espacio puede cooperar a la concentración de la actividad.

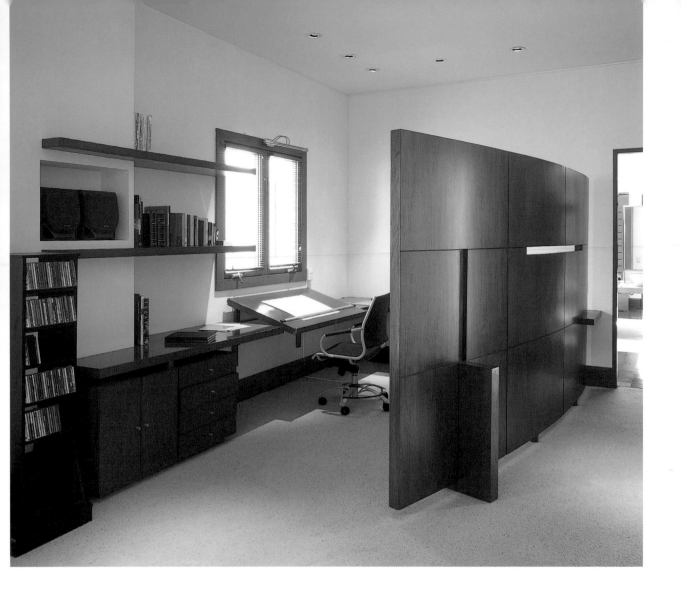

LORSQUE LES SALLES DE SEJOUR ET À MANGER ont de grandes baies vitrées qui permettent la vue vers l'extérieur, on peut établir un rapport de continuité entre l'intérieur et l'extérieur, profiter du paysage et favoriser l'entrée de lumière naturelle. Ces éléments deviennent parfois des cadres vitaux dynamiques qui offrent aux usagers une sensation de plus grande ampleur. Quant aux lieux de travail ou d'étude, l'emploi de portes rembourrées ou de murs qui dédoublent l'espace permet de s'isoler partiellement ou totalement et, par là même, de se concentrer.

WENN DAS WOHNZIMMER und das EßZIMMER große Kristalloberflächen haben, die dass Vergegenwärtigung zum Exterieur erlauben, kann man eine Verbindung innen-externer Kontinuität gründen, die Landschaft richtig anschauen und damit kann die natürliches Licht einkommen. Diese Elemente sind wichtig, sie bringen dynamische und lebenswichtige Quadrate und auch eine Sensation von grössere Weite. Die partielle oder totale Isoliertheit durch die Verwendung von Lampen oder Mauern, die den Raum unterteilen kann im Fall der Arbeitszimmer zur Konzentration der Aktivität kooperieren.

IN DIRECT CONTRAST with the ideas promoted by the Functionalist Movement, which proposed a strict sense of unity, in recent years, with regard to the architectural project in general and the peculiarities of interior design, there has been an important trend towards considering the criteria of unity in diversity. And so, it is feasible and accepted to combine furniture and objects from different styles.

A CONTRACORRIENTE con las ideas promovidas por el Movimiento Funcionalista, que proponía un estricto sentido de unidad, en los últimos años, tanto en lo que se refiere al proyecto arquitectónico en lo general como lo que tiene que ver con las particularidades del diseño de interiores, ha sido importante la tendencia que sugiere la consideración del criterio de unidad en la variedad. Así las cosas, es factible y aceptado combinar muebles y objetos que pueden ser de estilos diferentes.

À CONTRE-COURANT des idées promues par le Mouvement Fonctionnaliste, lequel proposait un sens strict d'unité, ces dernières années, la tendance qui suggère la prise en compte du critère d'unité dans la variété a acquis de l'importance, tant en ce qui concerne le projet architectonique en général qu'en ce qui concerne les particularités du plan et design d'intérieurs. Il est donc possible et acceptable de combiner des meubles et des objets de styles différents.

IM GEGENTEIL mit die Ideen, die durch die Funktionalistische Bewegung in den letzten Jahren vorgeschlagen wurden, die Schlug einen strengen Einheitsinn, sowie für architektonischen Projekt im allgemeinen sonder auch im Interieur Design, ist die Tendenz, die die Überlegung des Einheitkriteriums in der Vielfalt vorschlägt wichtig geworden. Dieser Weg, die Kombination von Möbel und Gegenständen anderer Stile ist durchführbar und akzeptabel.

Compositions organized and expressed through a
play on levels, lacking ornaments, with clear surfaces
finished in light colors, combined with large transparent
screens establishing a direct relationship and experience
between interior and exterior spaces can, as a whole,
be translated in neutral spaces that allow for the free
combination of furniture, paintings or sculptures of
different colors and textures.

Las composiciones que se organizan y expresan por medio
de juegos de planos, carentes de adornos, con superficies
tersas, terminadas en colores claros, combinadas con
amplias pantallas transparentes, estableciendo una
relación y vivencia directa entre espacios interiores y
exteriores, se pueden en conjunto traducir en espacios
neutros que posibilitan la libre combinación de muebles,
pinturas o esculturas, de distintos colores y texturas.

Les compositions, qui s'organisent et s'expriment grâce
à des jeux de plans, dépourvues d'ornements, aux
surfaces lisses et couleurs claires, assorties à de grands
écrans transparents, établissant ainsi un rapport et un lien
directs entre les espaces intérieurs et extérieurs, peuvent
se traduire en espaces neutres qui permettent la libre
combinaison de meubles, de peintures ou sculptures de
couleurs et textures diverses.

Die Kompositionen, die organisiert sind und mittels
flache Sets ausdrücken Dekorationen Fehlen, mit glatten
Oberflächen, beendet in klaren Farben, mit breiten
durchsichtigen Bildschirmen kombiniert, eine Verbindung
und direkte Erfahrung zwischen Interieur und Exterieur
Räumen gründen. Diese Fläche sind neutrale Räume, die
die freie Kombination von Möbel, Gemälde oder Skulpturen
mit anderen Farben und Texturen erleichtern.

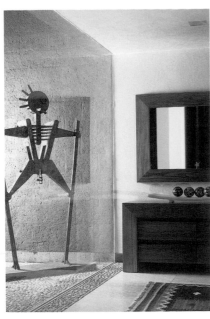

Sculpture can become a complement for architecture, and it is desirable from the beginning to know its characteristics and location for creating the proper space and lighting conditions.

La escultura se puede convertir en un complemento para la arquitectura, siendo deseable desde un principio conocer sus características y ubicación, de tal suerte de crearle las condiciones adecuadas de espacio y luz.

La sculpture peut devenir un complément de l'architecture si l'on connaît, dès le départ, ses caractéristiques et son emplacement, afin de créer les conditions adéquates d'espace et de lumière.

Die Skulptur kann ein Komplement für die Architektur werden. Seit dem Anfang sollte man die Merkmale und Lokalisierung kennen, um die geeigneten Räume und Lichtzustände zu kreieren.

Understanding that the quantity, quality and arrangement of the furniture is related to the size and characteristics of the space contributes to creating comfortable and harmonic atmospheres.

Comprender que la cantidad, calidad y disposición del mobiliario con el que se cuente está en relación con el tamaño y las cualidades del espacio, coopera a crear atmósferas confortables y armónicas.

Comprendre que la quantité, la qualité et la disposition du mobilier que l'on a est en rapport avec la taille et les qualités de l'espace, favorise la création de cadres confortables et harmonieux.

Verstehen daß die Quantität, Qualität und Disposition des Möbel im Zusammenhang mit der Größe und den Qualitäten des Raumes kooperiert zu die Gründung eine bequeme und harmonische Atmosphäre.

It is interesting to use surfaces that act as a background and create a contrast with the ornamental elements placed upon them.

Es interesante recurrir al uso de superficies que sirvan de fondo y creen contraste con los elementos decorativos que se coloquen sobre ellas.

Il est intéressant d'utiliser des surfaces qui servent de fond et qui créent un contraste avec les éléments décoratifs posés sur elles.

Es ist interessant, Oberflächen für Boden zu benutzen und Kontrast, die über den Oberflächen setzen, mit den dekorativen Elementen zu kreieren.

The design expressed by repetitive elements allows for maintaining a rhythm in the space; if the use of materials with personality is added to the multiplication of units, the space gains strength and liveliness.

El diseño que se expresa a través de elementos repetitivos permite mantener un ritmo en el espacio; si a la multiplicación de unidades se le suma el uso de materiales con carácter, el espacio adquiere fuerza y vitalidad.

Le plan et design qui s'exprime par des éléments répétitifs permet de maintenir un rythme dans l'espace. Celui-ci acquiert force et vitalité si, en plus de la multiplication d'unités, on y ajoute des matériaux qui ont du caractère.

Durch wiederholende Elemente des Design behält einen Rhythmus im Raum; wenn die Verwendung von Materialien mit Stil zur Multiplikation von Einheiten hinzugefügt wird, der Raum erwirbt Macht und Energie.

Within an austere ambiance, in which the artificial and the natural can be mixed visually and experientially, a few, well-selected elements may be enough for providing meaning, warmth and functionality to a given space. This idea is complemented if light colors, natural stones, wood and clay elements are used, combining them as objects and furniture related at the same time to tradition and modernity.

Dentro de un ambiente austero, en el que se puede mezclar visual y vivencialmente lo construido y lo natural, pocos elementos bien seleccionados pueden ser suficientes para darle sentido, calidez y funcionalidad a un espacio determinado. Esta idea se complementa si se utilizan colores claros, piedras naturales, componentes de madera y barro, a través de su combinación con objetos y mobiliario que se relacionen al mismo tiempo con la tradición y la modernidad.

Dans un cadre austère, dans lequel on peut mélanger de manière visuelle et expérimentale le construit et le naturel, peu d'éléments, bien sélectionnés, peuvent suffire pour donner un sens, de la chaleur et une fonctionnalité à un espace donné. On peut compléter cette idée en utilisant des couleurs claires, des pierres naturelles, des composants du bois et de la terre cuite, à travers la combinaison avec des objets et du mobilier qui se réfèrent à la fois à la tradition et à la modernité.

In einer strengen Atmosphäre, wo das Visual und die Lebhaftigkeit des Bau und die natürliche Sachen mischen, wenigen und ausgewälten Elementen geben Wärme, Funktionalität und einem bestimmten Sinn zu die Raum. Man kann diese Idee ergänzen, wenn klare Farben, natürliche Steine, hölzerne und schlammige Bestandteile benutzt werden, und solten auch ihre Kombination in Gegenständen und Möbel gleichzeitig mit der Tradition und der Modernität verbunden sein.

dining rooms comedores salles à manger eßzimmer

GENERATING ORIGINAL SPACES that multiply the occupant's sensory experiences has become a sign of the times. For this purpose, mixing furniture styles, and the combination of lighting and accessories, are used. But, no matter how eclectic an interior space, it is better not to abuse the shapes; their continuity, combined with the proper selection of color palettes and plays of light, help in obtaining attractive designs. A touch of color on a piece of furniture may be more striking and less taxing for the eye than the abuse of shapes.

GENERAR ESPACIOS ORIGINALES, que multipliquen las sensaciones de los usuarios, se ha convertido en un signo de actualidad. Para ello se recurre a la mezcla de estilos en muebles, combinaciones de iluminación y accesorios. Pero, por ecléctico que sea un interior, es conveniente no abusar de las formas; la continuidad de éstas aunada a la selección adecuada de gamas cromáticas y a juegos de luz ayudan a obtener diseños atractivos. El toque de color en algún mueble puede ser más contundente y menos cansado a la vista, que el abuso de formas.

GENERER DES ESPACES ORIGINAUX, qui multiplient les sensations des usagers, est devenu un signe actuel. Pour cela, on a recours au mélange de styles des meubles et aux combinaisons d'éclairage et d'accessoires. Mais, si éclectique que soit un intérieur, il convient de ne pas abuser des formes; en effet, leur continuité alliée à la sélection adéquate de gammes chromatiques et à des jeux de lumière aident à obtenir des designs attrayants. Une touche de couleur sur un meuble peut être plus frappante et moins fatigante pour la vue que l'excès de formes.

DIE GENERATION VON ORIGINALEN RÄUMEN, die den Sensationen der Benutzer vervielfacht, ist ein Stil der Aktualität. Um dieses zu erreichen verwenden wir die Mischung von Stilen in Möbel, Kombinationen von Illumination und Zubehöre. Aber es ist zweckmäßig den Formen nicht mißzubrauchen; die geeignete Auswahl chromatischer Ausmaße, die Kontinuität der Formen und das Licht bilden attraktive Designs. Die bunte Berührung in Möbel überwältigt mehr und es ermüdet weniger die Sicht als die falsche Anwendung in Formen.

THE DEVELOPMENT OF MODERN TECHNOLOGY has had an impact in our idea on the design of a house. Now we can build houses that previously would have seemed unthinkable. Building materials and techniques are constantly renewed. Nowadays there is a academic specialization on the subject of design. While there are architects capable of approaching different design issues, there also are those who are exclusively devoted to home design, as well as experts that only deal with exterior or interior spaces, such as kitchens, dining rooms or bathrooms. There is similar specialization among suppliers of materials and furniture.

EL DESARROLLO DE LA TECNOLOGÍA MODERNA ha impactado nuestra idea del diseño de una casa. Se pueden construir viviendas que antes parecían impensables. Materiales y técnicas constructivas se renuevan constantemente. En nuestros días existe una especialización en materia de diseño. Si bien existen arquitectos capaces de enfrentar distintos temas de diseño, también hay los que se dedican exclusivamente al diseño de casas, así como expertos que se ocupan solamente de los espacios exteriores o interiores, tales como cocinas, comedores o baños. Algo semejante sucede con los proveedores de materiales y muebles.

LE DEVELOPPEMENT DE LA TECHNOLOGIE MODERNE a eu un fort impact sur la conception du design d'une maison. On peut construire des logements qui, auparavant, paraissaient impensables. Les matériaux et les techniques de construction se renouvellent constamment. De nos jours, il existe une spécialisation en matière de design. Quoiqu'il y ait des architectes capables de faire face à divers thèmes de design, il y en a d'autres qui se consacrent exclusivement au design de maisons, et il y a aussi des experts qui s'occupent uniquement des espaces extérieurs ou intérieurs, comme les cuisines, les salles à manger ou les salles de bains. Un phénomène similaire a lieu en ce qui concerne les fournisseurs de matériaux et de meubles.

DIE ENTWICKLUNG DER MODERNEN TECHNOLOGIE hat unsere Idee vom Design eines Hauses beeinflußt. Häuser, die vor einige Jahren undenkbar waren können jetzt gebaut werden. Materialen und konstruktive Techniken werden ständig erneuert. Jetzt existiert eine Spezialisierung für das Design. Es gibt fähigen Architekten, die verschiedene Designthemen gegenüberzustehen, sowie Leute, die ausschließlich Häuser entwerfen, und Experten in Verantwortung von außern oder inneren Räumen, wie Küchen, Eßzimmer oder Badezimmer. Etwas ähnliches passiert zu den Lieferanten der Materialien und Möbel.

For the places where bread and salt is shared, the predominance of complementary furniture and accessories is commonly and openly accepted, using wood elements, combined with other materials such as glass or fabric to generate a comfortable atmosphere.

Para los lugares donde se comparte el pan y la sal, es usual y abiertamente aceptado el predominio de muebles y accesorios complementarios, la utilización de componentes de madera, combinados con otros materiales como el cristal o las telas para propiciar una atmósfera confortable.

Pour les lieux où l'on partage le pain, la prédominance de meubles et d'accessoires complémentaires, et l'utilisation de composants du bois, alliés à d'autres matériaux comme le cristal ou le tissu pour favoriser un cadre confortable, sont habituellement et ouvertement acceptées.

Für das Eßzimmer und ähnliche Räume ist das Vorherrschen von Möbel und komplementären Zubehöre üblich und akzeptiert. Sowie die Verwendung hölzerner Bestandteile, in Kombination mit anderen Materialien als Kristall oder Stoffe, um eine bequeme Atmosphäre zu erzeugen.

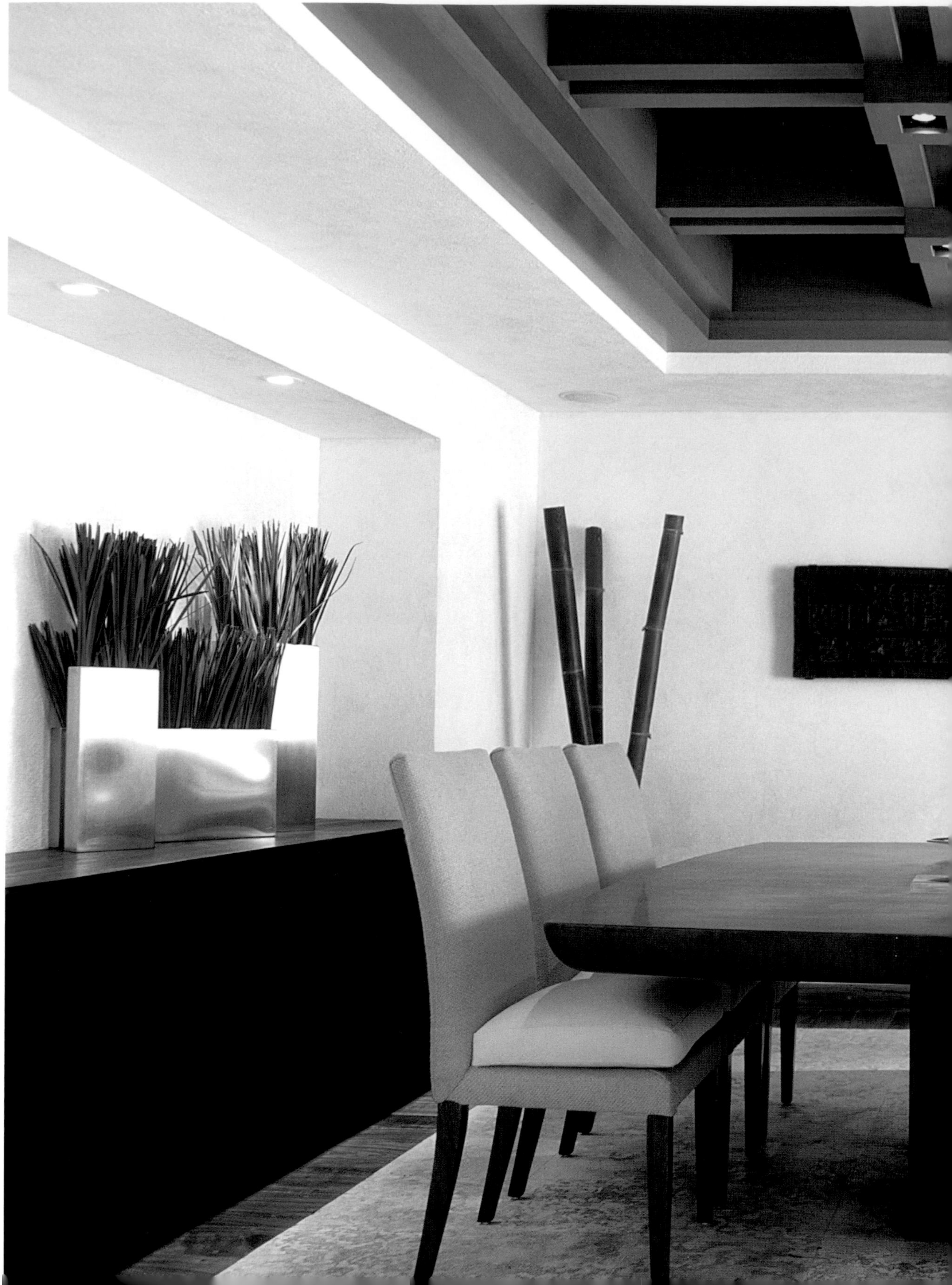

Sometimes the contrast suggested by the simple and abstract shapes that dominate the design of a space may be interesting and may be expressed by using a unitary material such as marble, and the ornamental objects with shapes that may refer to certain elements that mimic the qualities of nature.

En algunas ocasiones puede resultar interesante el contraste que se sugiere entre las formas simples y abstractas que dominan en el diseño de un espacio y que se pueden expresar a través del manejo de un material unitario como puede ser el mármol, y los objetos decorativos cuyas formas pueden estar referidas a ciertos elementos que imitan los rasgos de la naturaleza.

Parfois, il peut être intéressant de contraster les formes simples et abstraites qui dominent dans le plan et design d'un espace et qui peuvent s'exprimer par l'emploi d'un matériel unitaire, tel que le marbre, et d'objets décoratifs dont les formes peuvent correspondre à certains éléments qui imitent les caractéristiques de la nature.

Manchmal, die Kontraste zwischen einfachen und abstrakten Formen resultieren interessanten. Diese Formen dominieren im Design eines Raumes und, daß durch die Verwendung eines einheitlichen Materials ausgedrückt werden können wie zum Beispiel der Marmor und die dekorativen Gegenstände, wessen Formen bestimmte Elemente, die die Merkmale der Natur imitieren.

baths
baños
salles de bains
badezimmer

THE EVOLUTION that has taken place in the area of design criteria for bathroom spaces never ceases to surprise, these are spaces where even aspects that go beyond their strict operational function are considered. Nowadays bathrooms can be very large, include areas for keeping linen, contain places designed for activities related to grooming and even exercise devices. Furthermore, technology has allowed the use of covering materials with large pieces that reduce the number of seams, providing a better look and making cleaning easier.

NO DEJA DE SORPRENDER la evolución que ha habido en cuanto a los criterios de diseño para los espacios destinados a baños, en los que, incluso, se consideran aspectos que van más allá de su estricta función operativa. Hoy en día los baños pueden ser muy amplios, incluir áreas de guardado de blancos o contener lugares diseñados para realizar las actividades propias del arreglo personal. Además, la tecnología ha permitido el uso de materiales de recubrimiento con piezas grandes que reducen el número de juntas, brindando una mejor apariencia y facilitando su limpieza.

L'EVOLUTION dans les critères du plan et design des espaces destinés aux salles de bains, ne cesse de surprendre. On prend d'ailleurs en compte des aspects qui dépassent leur simple fonction opératoire. De nos jours, les salles de bains peuvent être spacieuses, inclure des coins pour ranger le linge, contenir des endroits planifiés pour réaliser les activités liées à la toilette et même disposer d'appareils pour faire de l'exercice. De plus, la technologie permet l'emploi de matériaux de recouvrement dont les grandes pièces réduisent le nombre de joints, et offre ainsi une meilleure apparence et facilite leur nettoyage.

DIE EVOLUTION des Design für die Räume der Badezimmer überrascht uns immer. Jenseits betrachten diese Aspekten eine strenge wirksame Funktion. Jetzt können die Badezimmer sehr breit sein, können Räume für Wandschränke einbeziehen, haben Räume, die entworfen wurden, um persönliche Aktivitäten auszuführen, und enthalten auch Apparate für Training. Die Technologie hat auch die Verwendung von Belagmaterialien mit großen Stücken erlaubt. Diese Technologie bieten ein besseres Aussehen an und erleichtern das Reinigen.

Industrial design applied to bathroom furniture and accessories has generated a broad variety that allows for achieving countless variations, which, added to the general design of the bathroom, make it easier to customize the design.

El diseño industrial aplicado a muebles y accesorios de baño ha generado un amplio repertorio que permite lograr un sinnúmero de variantes, mismas que sumadas al diseño general del baño facilitan personalizar los diseños.

Le design industriel appliqué aux meubles et accessoires de bain a généré un vaste répertoire qui permet d'obtenir un grand nombre de variantes qui, ajoutées au plan et design général de la salle de bains, facilitent la personnalisation des plans et designs.

Das industrielle Design für Möbel und Badezimmerzubehöre hat ein breites Repertoire erzeugt. Das Repertoire erlaubt das Erreichen von vielen Varianten, welcher zum allgemeinen Design des Badezimmern hinzu fügen.

Bathroom accessories and furniture are sometimes used as sculptures meant for personal hygiene.

Los accesorios y muebles de baño llegan a utilizarse como objetos escultóricos dedicados al aseo personal.

Les accessoires et meubles de bain s'utilisent parfois comme objets sculpturaux consacrés à l'hygiène personnelle.

Die Zubehöre und Badezimmer-Möbel werden in ihrem Design als bildhauerische Gegenstände, die für persönlichen Reinlichkeit benutzt ist.

TERRACES TYPICALLY function as spatial extensions of dining or living spaces. Sometimes out on the open air and sometimes covered or relatively protected by pergolas, partially shaded, they generate an informal and relaxed ambiance. These are spaces that often have multifunctional purposes. The treatments of its finishing uses wood fit for outdoor use, combining it in the same way with the design of the furniture, achieve a warm and comfortable ambiance.

GENERALMENTE LAS TERRAZAS operan como extensiones espaciales de los lugares de comer o convivencia. A veces a cielo abierto y otras cubiertas o protegidas relativamente por pérgolas, en la semi-sombra, propician un ambiente informal y relajado. Se trata de espacios que suelen tener un carácter multifuncional. Los tratamientos de sus acabados empleando maderas propias para uso en exteriores, combinando en este mismo sentido con los diseños de su mobiliario, logran un ambiente cálido y confortable.

EN GENERAL, LES TERRASSES fonctionnent comme des extensions spatiales des lieux de restauration ou de vie commune. Soit à ciel ouvert, soit couvertes, soit protégées en partie par des pergolas, à demi-ombragées, elles favorisent un cadre relâché et relaxant. Ce sont des espaces qui ont d'ordinaire un caractère multifonctionnel. Les traitements de leurs finitions, si on emploie des bois propres aux extérieurs, et si on les combine avec le plan et design de son mobilier, contribuent à un cadre chaleureux et confortable.

GEWÖHNLICH SIND DIE TERRASSEN Raumvergrößerungen des Eßzimmer oder Wohnzimmer. Unbedeckt, gedeckt, durch Pergolas geschützt oder im halb-Schatten bringen diese Terrassen eine zwanglose und entspannte Atmosphäre. Eine warme und bequeme Atmosphäre wird, durch Holzenden für Verwendung in Exterieur und in Kombination mit dem Design des Möbel, erreichen.

terraces
terrazas
terrasses
terrassen

CONSIDERING THE POTENTIAL RESTRICTIONS when it comes to space that a house may have, the option of using the rooftops as terraces was created. This idea has spread and nowadays using the rooftops is considered, from its inception, in the design of many houses.

Terraces on rooftops allow for more generous and immediate contact with the sky and the surrounding environment, becoming a gathering space within a private ambiance.

CONSIDERANDO LAS POSIBLES LIMITACIONES en materia de espacio que suelen existir en una casa, se creó la modalidad de aprovechar las superficies de las azoteas como terrazas. Esta idea se ha generalizado y hoy en día en el diseño de muchas viviendas se toma en cuenta, desde su fase de concepción, la utilización de los techos.

Las terrazas en azotea permiten tener un contacto más generoso e inmediato con el cielo y con el entorno circundante, convirtiéndose en un sitio de reunión dentro de un ambiente de privacidad.

ETANT DONNE LES LIMITATIONS spatiales qui existent généralement dans une maison, la tendance est de profiter des superficies des toits plats pour en faire des terrasses. Cette idée s'est généralisée et de nos jours, dans le plan et design de beaucoup de logements, on prend en compte, dès leur conception, l'utilisation des toits.

Les terrasses sur les toits permettent d'avoir un contact plus généreux et immédiat avec le ciel et avec l'environnement, elles deviennent ainsi un lieu de réunion dans un cadre privé.

WEGEN DER MÖGLICHEN Raumgrenze eines Hauses, wurde die Oberfläche der Dächer als Terrassen benutzt. Diese Idee ist verallgemeinert worden und ist jetzt seit der Konzeptionphase die Verwendung der Dächer aufgenomen.

Die Terrassen in Dach erlauben einen großzügigeren und unmittelbareren Kontakt mit dem Himmel und mit der Umgebung, wie ein Treffpunkt in einer privaten Atmosphäre.

Understanding the surroundings, which may be abstract or intimately linked to elements of nature, is fundamental to properly undertake the design of a terrace.

Comprender el entorno, que puede ser un tanto abstracto o íntimamente vinculado con elementos de la naturaleza, es fundamental para afrontar correctamente el diseño de una terraza.

Comprendre le milieu ambiant, qui peut être un peu abstrait ou intimement lié à des éléments de la nature, est fondamental pour élaborer convenablement le plan et design d'une terrasse.

Um eine Terrasse korrekt zu entwerfen, muss muss man die Umgebung kennen; manchmal abstrakt, manchmal mit Elementen der Natur zusammengefügt.

The selection of the furniture to be used on a terrace should be conducted with care, with an attempt to match it with the spatial atmosphere that is the result of the whole architectural design. The material qualities of the place, its textures and the resulting scale influence the decision.

La selección del mobiliario a emplearse en una terraza debería realizarse con cuidado, intentando hacerla corresponder con la atmósfera espacial que resulta del diseño arquitectónico general. Influyen en la decisión las calidades de materiales del lugar, sus texturas y la escala resultante.

La sélection du mobilier à employer dans une terrasse devrait se faire soigneusement, pour que celle-ci soit en harmonie avec le cadre ambiant qui ressort du plan et design architectonique général. Les qualités des matériaux du lieu, leurs textures et l'échelle influent sur cette décision.

Die Auswahl des Möbel für eine Terrasse sollte vorsichtig ausgeführt werden, es sollte mit der Raumatmosphäre des allgemeinen architektonischen Entwurfes korrespondieren. Die Qualität des Material in dem Ort, die Texturen und der resultierend Maßstab beeinflussen in der Entscheidung.

CREDITS • CRÉDITOS • CRÉDITS • KREDITE

architectonic
arquitectónicos
architectoniques
architektonische

a. coello, (top right and bottom left) ARTECK, francisco guzmán giraud y alejandro bernardi, (bottom right) ABAX, fernando de haro, jesús fernández y omar fuentes ● **133** (top left) miguel campero y josé luis salamanca, (top right) francisco guzmán giraud, (bottom left) alejandro bernardi ● **134 - 135** C'CUBICA, emilio cabrero, andrea cesarman y marco a. coello ● **136 - 137** jaime guzmán y fernando ogarrio ● **138** (top right) GRUPO CONSTRUCTOR MAR, ricardo martínez de alva y ernesto martínez de alva, (top center) CASAS DE MÉXICO, jaime gómez vázquez y josé manuel gómez castellanos, (top right, center right and bottom left) PML ARQUITECTOS, pablo martínez lanz, (center left and bottom right) ABAX, fernando de haro, jesús fernández y omar fuentes, (center) ARENA ARQUITECTOS, jaime arena, (bottom center) GRUPO ARQUITECH, juan josé sánchez-aedo y josé luis quiroz ● **139** GÓMEZ + GÓMEZ ARQS., césar gómez gómez ● **140** GANTOUS ARQUITECTOS, claudio gantous y christian gantous ● **141** jaime guzmán y fernando ogarrio ● **142** (left) ABAX, fernando de haro, jesús fernández y omar fuentes ● **142 - 143** ARTECK, francisco guzmán giraud y alejandro bernardi ● **145** (top) ART ARQUITECTOS ASOCIADOS, antonio rueda ventosa, (bottom) ARTECK, francisco guzmán giraud y alejandro bernardi ● **146** (top left) francisco guzmán giraud, (top right) ABAX, fernando de haro, jesús fernández y omar fuentes, (bottom) MODA IN CASA, louis poiré ● **147** (top) ARTECK, francisco guzmán giraud y alejandro bernardi, (bottom) TERRÉS, javier valenzuela, fernando valenzuela y guillermo valenzuela ● **148** (left) RIVADENEYRA ARQUITECTOS, alejandro rivadeneyra, (right) ABAX, fernando de haro, jesús fernández y omar fuentes ● **149** (left) UNIDAD DISEÑO, mario lazo, (right) jaime guzmán y fernando ogarrio ● **150** C-CHIC, olga musalli h. y sara mizrahi ● **151** jaime guzmán y fernando ogarrio ● **152** C'CUBICA, emilio cabrero, andrea cesarman y marco a. coello ● **153** jaime guzmán y fernando ogarrio ● **154** (top) MARQCÓ DISEÑO, mariangel álvarez y covadonga hernández, (center) MM ÁLVAREZ INTERIORES, margarita álvarez y juan j. zapata álvarez, (bottom) GRUPO BAI, max betancourt suárez ● **155** MARQCÓ DISEÑO, mariangel álvarez y covadonga hernández ● **156 - 157** C'CUBICA, emilio cabrero, andrea cesarman y marco a. coello ● **158** DIM ING. & ARQS. carlos dayan, isidoro dayan y eduardo dayan ● **158 - 159** PIACERE Y PAYEN ARQUITECTOS, jacques payen ● **159** GRUPO ARQUITECTOMA, francisco martín del campo y josé portilla ● **160 - 161** HAJJ DESIGN LESS ● **162** PIACERE Y ROJKIND ARQUITECTOS, michel rojkind ● **163** HAJJ DESIGN LESS ● **165** (top) ABAX, fernando de haro, jesús fernández y omar fuentes, (bottom) LÓPEZ BAZ Y CALLEJA ● **166 - 167** AGRAZ ARQUITECTOS, ricardo agraz ● **168** GANTOUS ARQUITECTOS, claudio gantous y christian gantous ● **168 - 169** (left) GANTOUS ARQUITECTOS, claudio gantous y christian gantous ● **169** F.V.A ARQUITECTOS, jesús ferreiro ● **170** LÓPEZ BAZ Y CALLEJA ● **171** GA ARQUITECTOS, daniel álvarez ● **172** (left) ABAX, fernando de haro, jesús fernández y omar fuentes ● **172 - 173** LÓPEZ-GUERRA ARQS. - MUSEOTEC, francisco lópez-guerra almada ● **173** (right) GA ARQUITECTOS, daniel álvarez ● **174** LÓPEZ BAZ Y CALLEJA ● **175** ARQUITECTUM, alberto crespo huerta ● **176 - 177** LÓPEZ BAZ Y CALLEJA ● **178** (top left) ARTECK, francisco guzmán giraud y alejandro bernardi, (bottom right) marco aldaco, (top right and bottom left) TERRÉS, javier valenzuela, fernando valenzuela y guillermo valenzuela ● **179** (top left) MARTÍNEZ-SORDO, juan salvador martínez y luis martín sordo, (top right) jaime guzmán y fernando ogarrio, (bottom left) MARQCÓ DISEÑO, mariangel álvarez y covadonga hernández ● **180** (top) francisco guzmán giraud, (bottom) TALLER B, enrique bardasano ● **181** (top) MIGDAL ARQUITECTOS, jaime varon, abraham metta y alex metta, (bottom) ABAX, fernando de haro, jesús fernández y omar fuentes ● **182 - 183** MM ÁLVAREZ INTERIORES, margarita álvarez y juan j. zapata álvarez ● **184** (top left) ARTECK, francisco guzmán giraud y alejandro bernardi, (top right) DIM ING. & ARQS. carlos dayan y diego casanova, (bottom) ABAX, fernando de haro, jesús fernández y omar fuentes ● **186** (left) francisco guzmán giraud, (left) RIVADENEYRA ARQUITECTOS, alejandro rivadeneyra ● **187** (left) jaime guzmán y fernando ogarrio, (right) CASAS DE MÉXICO, jaime gómez vázquez y josé manuel gómez castellanos ● **188** francisco guzmán giraud ● **189** jaime guzmán y fernando ogarrio ● **190** (top) ARTECK, francisco guzmán giraud y alejandro bernardi, (bottom) benjamín gonzález y jorge covarrubias ● **191** (top) ARTECK, francisco guzmán giraud y alejandro bernardi, (bottom) CASAS DE MÉXICO, jaime gómez vázquez y josé manuel gómez castellanos ● **192** (top left) RIVADENEYRA ARQUITECTOS, alejandro rivadeneyra, (top right and bottom) C'CUBICA, emilio cabrero, andrea cesarman y marco a. coello ● **193** (top) DIM ING. & ARQS. carlos dayan y diego casanova, (bottom) UNIDAD DISEÑO, mario lazo ● **194** (bottom) SORDO MADALENO ARQS. javier sordo madaleno ● **194 - 195** (top and bottom)

photographic
fotográficos
photographiques
fotografische

Se terminó de imprimir en el mes de Abril del 2005 en
Hong Kong. El cuidado de la edición estuvo a cargo de
AM Editores S.A. de C.V.